Preparing for the Drug (Free) Years:
A Family Activity Book

Developed by
Developmental Research and Programs, Inc.
J. David Hawkins
Richard F. Catalano
Edward O. Brown
Patricia F. Vadasy

and

Roberts, Fitzmahan & Associates
Clay Roberts
Don Fitzmahan
Neal Starkman
Melissa Ransdell

Prepared Under the Supervision of
Comprehensive Health Education Foundation
Carl Nickerson
Jay Schupack

Acknowledgments

We gratefully thank:

Sharry Heckt, Barbara Daugherty, Sharon Tate-Laine, and Mary Goehring, of the Washington State Substance Abuse Coalition;

Elliot Herman, developer of Refusal Skills®;

Kathleen Burgoyne and Gwendolyn Jones of the Seattle Social Development Project;

Louise Benaltabe, Production Coordinator, Comprehensive Health Education Foundation;

The Davis Group, cover design and design consultants; and

Nancy Gellos, illustrator

all of whose sound and practical advice and concern for children made this a better book.

© 1987, 1988 Developmental Research and Programs, Inc.; Roberts, Fitzmahan & Associates, Inc.; Comprehensive Health Education Foundation (CHEF®)

Second Edition — 1988

4/92   15K

ISBN 0-935529-03-9

We dedicate this book to our families.

Contents

How to Use This Book

This book is more than a book; it's also a tool and a toy. Use it like you'd use a tool to build a house, and play with it like you'd play with a toy of endless variations. What can this book do?

▶ It can help you build a stronger, closer, happier family.

▶ It can help you reduce the risk of your children's getting into trouble with drugs.

▶ It can show you ways to have fun as a family.

You'll notice tear-out sheets in the back of each chapter. Use them. Have fun with them. We developed *Preparing for the Drug (Free) Years: A Family Activity Book* so that you'd have a little information to read and a lot of activities to do.

This book is for families. There are many kinds of families: families with one adult and those with more; families with one child and those

with more; families with stepparents; adoptive families; extended families; families who are rural and urban, rich and poor; families of all different colors and sizes and shapes. Which kinds of families can benefit from this book? If in your home at least one adult is responsible for at least one child; if the people who live with you depend on each other for any kind of emotional, financial, or social support; and if you genuinely care for one another, then you can benefit from this book. The important thing is to recognize that your family can be an effective force for preventing your child from using drugs.

Some of you are using this book as part of a program for parents called "Preparing for the Drug (Free) Years." The program features a series of workshops at which parents of children in grades 4 through 7 get information and develop skills in five major topics: confronting the problem of children's use of drugs; developing a clear family position on drugs; teaching children skills to help them stay out of trouble; containing family conflict; and strengthening family bonds. If you'd like to learn more about "Preparing for the Drug (Free) Years," or if you'd like to learn about the specific risks that contribute to the likelihood a child will have a problem with drugs, please write or call Developmental Research and Programs, Inc., at the following address and phone number:

Developmental Research and Programs, Inc.
130 Nickerson Street, Suite 107
Seattle, WA 98109
(206) 286-1805

Others of you are using this book as a supplement to a drug education curriculum, such as *Here's Looking At You, 2000*®. This comprehensive K-12 curriculum conveys information about drugs and chemical dependency, teaches social skills like staying out of trouble with friends, and promotes children's bonding to school and family. If you'd like to learn more about *Here's Looking At You, 2000,* please write or call Roberts, Fitzmahan & Associates, Inc. at the following address and phone number:

Roberts, Fitzmahan & Associates
9131 California Ave. S.W.
Seattle, Washington 98136-2599
(206) 932-8409

Finally, many of you saw this book at a bookstore or meeting and thought that it might address some of the concerns you have about your children's exposure to drugs. We think that it will, and we want you to know that *Preparing for the Drug (Free) Years: A Family Activity Book* can be used all by itself.

The book has six chapters. Chapter 6 is devoted to organizing a parent support group in your community. The other chapters focus on activities you can do with your family. In each of these chapters you'll find the following:

► an explanation of a topic important in reducing the risk of teenage drug abuse
► a step-by-step description of a process you can learn to help reduce the risks of your own child getting into trouble with drugs
► an easy-to-use agenda you can follow to hold a family meeting
► other activities relating to the topic you can do with your family
► tear-out "Familygrams" you can use to remind yourself what you're working on and

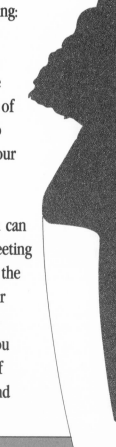

display around the house, for example, on refrigerator doors (These Familygrams are shown in miniature in the text to help you identify them and to make them easier to reproduce if they're used or lost).

In addition, we've provided you with three other pieces of information in the back of this book which we think you'll find helpful:

▶ a behavior checklist for children who may be using drugs
▶ a chart which categorizes federally controlled substances by how they're used and how they affect the user
▶ a list of organizations you can consult for further information about drug use

Practice what you learn in this book. Make up your own activities, or adapt the ones we've suggested to your own needs. Share the book with your friends and with other parents in your community. Use it as long as you get something out of it. As you grow and change, so do the activities in the book.

We repeat: You have in your hands a tool and a toy. But nobody ever built a house by staring at a hammer, and nobody ever had fun with a toy that stayed on the shelf. So don't just read: Participate. *You* are the most important part of this book.

Chapter One
Getting Started:
How to Prevent Drug Abuse in Your Family

Smoking a Joint

Chewing a Pinch of Tobacco

Sipping a Cup of Black Tea

Snorting a Line of Cocaine

Drinking a Can of Cold Beer

Shooting Up Heroin

All of the above are descriptions of the use of drugs—marijuana, nicotine, caffeine, cocaine, alcohol, heroin. Some of these drugs are illegal. Some are accepted by our society; you can pick up a magazine and read advertisements for them. All of these drugs change the way our minds and bodies function, but people have widely differing opinions on their use. What can you do about your children's use of these drugs? What *should* you do? The information in this book will help you decide.

You see the effects of drug abuse all around you—destroyed careers, broken homes, automobile accidents, deaths from overdose. You know that drug abuse is a bad thing, yet maybe you think that your child, a "good kid," would never get involved with drugs. Or maybe you think that using drugs is the furthest thing from your child's mind right now, and that there's plenty of time to talk about drugs when your child gets into high school.

Unfortunately, many "good kids" end up in trouble with drugs. And high school is about five years too late to begin making your child's teenage years drug-free.

That's why the information and activities in this book apply especially to families with children in grades 4 through 7. Children are most likely to be introduced to nicotine, alcohol, and marijuana in grades 6 through 9. More than half of the children who use these drugs first use them before they leave ninth grade—before they reach high school. According to recent studies released by the National Institute on Drug Abuse (1987), by the time students leave high school, 68% have already tried nicotine, 91% alcohol, and 51% marijuana.

You may have noticed that we've been referring to certain drugs more than others—nicotine, alcohol, and marijuana. That is because children who get in trouble with *any* drug most likely use nicotine, alcohol, and marijuana first, usually in that order. And, as we said, they start in grades 6 through 9. That is why it is so important to consider these three drugs when you are developing a strategy for preventing drug abuse in your family.

That means that most children face a decision about whether to use drugs while they are still in middle or junior high school. The data point out the importance of this decision: Children who use drugs before the age of 15 have a much greater risk of having serious problems with alcohol and other drugs than do children who don't use drugs by that age. So the time to prepare for the drug-free years is *now*, before your children face that decision.

Risk Factors
This book gives your family information and skills which can reduce the risks of your children having problems with drugs. Studies have shown that certain factors increase the risk that children will have problems with drugs. These factors are called "risk factors for teenage drug abuse." *Preparing for the Drug (Free) Years: A Family Activity Book*

helps you reduce the risks by addressing those risk factors.

Let's take a couple of examples to show you what we mean by "risk factors." Standing under a tree in an electrical storm is a risk factor for getting struck by lightning. Not everyone who stands under a tree in an electrical storm gets struck by lightning, and sometimes people who are not standing under trees get struck by lightning. But you know that standing under a tree during an electrical storm increases your risk of getting struck by lightning.

Another example: Smoking is a risk factor for getting lung cancer. Not everyone who smokes gets lung cancer, and some nonsmokers get lung cancer, but, again, you know that smoking increases your risk of getting lung cancer. You can reduce the risk of getting struck by lightning by not standing under trees in electrical storms, and you can reduce the risk of getting lung cancer by not smoking. When you know the risk factor, you can reduce the risk.

There are risk factors for drug abuse, too. The more risk

factors present, the greater the risk a child will have a problem with drugs. For example, "having friends who use drugs" is a risk factor for teenage drug abuse. A child whose friends use drugs has an increased risk of getting into trouble with drugs. As we said before, another risk factor for teenage drug abuse is "early first use of drugs." A child who begins to use drugs before age 15 has an increased risk of getting into trouble with drugs. This book identifies the known risk factors for teenage drug abuse, and helps you reduce the risks. Every activity in the book addresses at least one risk factor. Let's look at the other known risk factors for teenage drug abuse:

▶ family history of alcoholism
▶ family management problems
▶ parental drug use and positive parental attitudes toward use
▶ early antisocial behavior and hyperactivity
▶ academic failure beginning in middle to late elementary school
▶ little commitment to school
▶ alienation, rebelliousness, and lack of bonding to society

▶ antisocial behavior in early adolescence
▶ friends who use drugs
▶ favorable attitudes toward drug use
▶ early first use of drugs

Let's review each of these risk factors. Note which ones apply to *your* children. You may want to complete the risk factor check on the next page for each of your children.

1 Family history of alcoholism. When a family member has abused alcohol, boys in particular have a high risk for abusing alcohol themselves. Boys with alcoholic fathers are up to four times more likely to abuse alcohol themselves. This risk may be a result of biology as well as environment. On the biological side, there is evidence that some children of alcoholics have a genetic predisposition to alcoholism. On the environmental side, parents who are alcoholics provide a powerful role model for their children that is likely to influence their children's behavior.

2 Family management problems. In order to make good decisions about their behavior, children need to get from their family

"... standing under a tree in an electrical storm is a risk factor for getting struck by lightning ..."

Risk Check for Your Child

What's the risk that your child will abuse drugs? Complete this risk check to find out. Different children in the same family can have a different risk for drug abuse, so complete the check for each of your children. Place each child's initials in a column at the left and check the appropriate columns for each risk factor that applies.

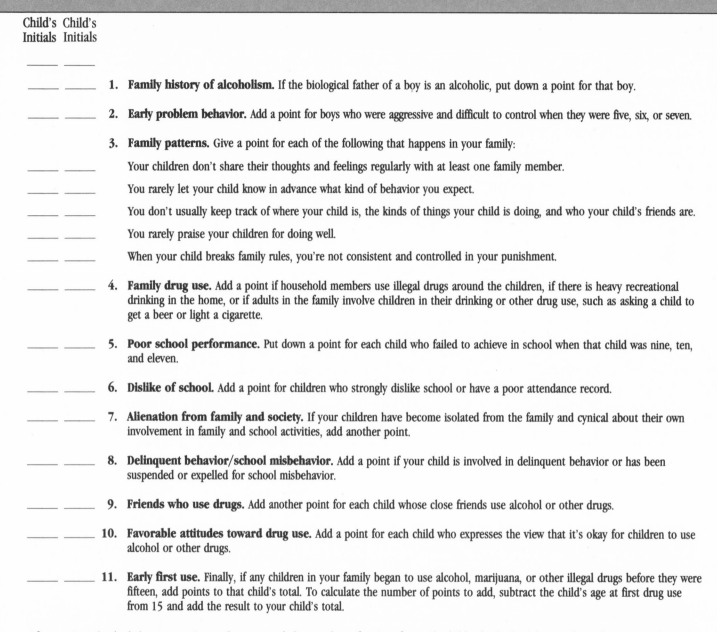

Child's Child's
Initials Initials

____ ____

____ ____ 1. **Family history of alcoholism.** If the biological father of a boy is an alcoholic, put down a point for that boy.

____ ____ 2. **Early problem behavior.** Add a point for boys who were aggressive and difficult to control when they were five, six, or seven.

3. **Family patterns.** Give a point for each of the following that happens in your family:

____ ____ Your children don't share their thoughts and feelings regularly with at least one family member.

____ ____ You rarely let your child know in advance what kind of behavior you expect.

____ ____ You don't usually keep track of where your child is, the kinds of things your child is doing, and who your child's friends are.

____ ____ You rarely praise your children for doing well.

____ ____ When your child breaks family rules, you're not consistent and controlled in your punishment.

____ ____ 4. **Family drug use.** Add a point if household members use illegal drugs around the children, if there is heavy recreational drinking in the home, or if adults in the family involve children in their drinking or other drug use, such as asking a child to get a beer or light a cigarette.

____ ____ 5. **Poor school performance.** Put down a point for each child who failed to achieve in school when that child was nine, ten, and eleven.

____ ____ 6. **Dislike of school.** Add a point for children who strongly dislike school or have a poor attendance record.

____ ____ 7. **Alienation from family and society.** If your children have become isolated from the family and cynical about their own involvement in family and school activities, add another point.

____ ____ 8. **Delinquent behavior/school misbehavior.** Add a point if your child is involved in delinquent behavior or has been suspended or expelled for school misbehavior.

____ ____ 9. **Friends who use drugs.** Add another point for each child whose close friends use alcohol or other drugs.

____ ____ 10. **Favorable attitudes toward drug use.** Add a point for each child who expresses the view that it's okay for children to use alcohol or other drugs.

____ ____ 11. **Early first use.** Finally, if any children in your family began to use alcohol, marijuana, or other illegal drugs before they were fifteen, add points to that child's total. To calculate the number of points to add, subtract the child's age at first drug use from 15 and add the result to your child's total.

After you've checked the appropriate columns, total the number of points for each child. The higher the number, the greater the risk of problems with alcohol or other drugs. But remember, this is not a scientific assessment of your family. These are only statistical probabilities. The presence of many risk factors doesn't condemn your children to be drug abusers, nor does a low score mean they will be free of problems. This risk check is intended simply to alert you to pay attention to these factors, and to make the extra effort needed to change patterns where necessary.

clear guidelines for acceptable and unacceptable behavior. They need to be taught basic skills, and they need to be provided with consistent support and rewards for acceptable behaviors as well as consistent but appropriate punishment for unacceptable behaviors. They also need to know that their parents care enough to monitor their behaviors so that rewards and punishments are applied fairly. Children who grow up in homes where rules are not clearly stated and enforced have difficulty knowing what is expected of them. If they aren't consistently rewarded for doing good things, then children don't know when they *are* doing good things, and aren't made to feel that their good behavior makes any difference. Similarly, if they aren't consistently and appropriately disciplined for doing bad things, then they don't experience the security they need to develop a sense of right and wrong and an ability to exercise their own judgment. If their parents don't make an effort to observe whether they're doing good or bad things, then any system of reward and punishment becomes less meaningful. These children have an increased risk of developing problems with alcohol and other drugs.

3 Parental drug use and positive parental attitudes toward use. Although most of the data available on parental drug use come from studies on the effects of alcohol, we know that parents' attitudes and behaviors related to drugs—just like their attitudes and behaviors related to other issues, like religion and politics—influence the attitudes and behaviors of their children. Parents are particularly likely to influence their children when they involve their children in their own drug-taking activities, for example, by asking their child to get a beer from the refrigerator, to light their cigarette, or to mix a drink. Children who are drawn into these activities are more likely to see themselves as future users. They're more likely to use drugs when they're young. And early use greatly increases the risk of trouble with drugs later.

Parents' attitudes about alcohol seem to influence their children's attitudes about other drugs. A survey conducted by researchers at the University of Washington found that ninth-grade children whose parents approved of their drinking under parental supervision were more likely to have used marijuana and to be using marijuana at the time than were children of parents who disapproved of drinking at home, supervised or not. Parents' approval of children's moderate drinking, even under parental supervision, appeared to increase the risk of children's use of marijuana.

4 Early antisocial behavior and hyperactivity. This risk factor has been identified for boys who in kindergarten through the second grade have a history of aggressiveness. The risk is especially significant when this aggressiveness is combined with shyness and withdrawal. These children may hit other children or slam doors in their teacher's face. About 40% of boys with these kinds of behavior patterns will develop delinquency or drug problems. This doesn't mean that if your son acts this way he will necessarily develop a drug problem. Unless something is done to help him control those behaviors, however, he is at increased risk for drug problems later in his life.

5 Academic failure beginning in middle to late elementary school. Children who do poorly in school in the fourth, fifth, and sixth grades have an increased risk of abusing drugs. Academic failure can have several causes. It may result when a child becomes bored with school and stops working and caring. It may result when a child has a learning disability. It may result when there is a poor match between a teacher and a student. Whatever the cause, those children who do poorly in school are more likely than successful students to turn to alcohol or other drugs in the following four to five years.

6 Little commitment to school. Another risk factor is a child's lack of interest in school. Students in grades 4 through 7 who lose interest in school, for whatever reason, have a greater risk of getting into trouble with drugs.

7 Alienation, rebelliousness, lack of bonding to society. Some children see themselves as standing apart from the rest of their peers. They adopt an "I don't care" attitude about school, and display their isolation from school or home. They're not bonded to their school, to their family, or to any other positive social institution, and so are more

"... parents' attitudes and behaviors related to drugs—just like their attitudes and behaviors related to other issues, like religion and politics—influence the attitudes and behaviors of their children."

9

susceptible to the influence of drug-using peers.

8 **Antisocial behavior in early adolescence.** This risk factor includes misbehaving in school, skipping school, and getting into fights with other children and exhibiting delinquent behavior. Children who engage in these behaviors are at increased risk for engaging in another socially undesirable behavior, drug abuse.

9 **Friends who use drugs.** This is a strong risk factor for adolescent drug abuse, and it operates independently of other risk factors. This means that even children who grow up without other risk factors but who associate with children who use drugs are at an increased risk for developing problems with drugs. This risk factor underscores the power of peer influence on teenagers.

10 **Favorable attitudes toward drug use.** When children are in the fourth, fifth, or sixth grade, they often have very strong feelings *against* drugs. They'll tell you how terrible cigarettes smell or how awful beer tastes. They think that children who use drugs are "stupid" or "losers."

Yet by the time these children enter junior high school, they may begin associating with peers who use drugs, and their attitudes can change quickly. This shift in attitudes often comes just before children begin to experiment with alcohol or other drugs.

11 **Early first use of drugs.** Most children who *do* try cigarettes, alcohol, and marijuana do so by the time they leave junior high school. By the time they leave high school, two out of three children drink alcohol at least once a month, one out of four smokes marijuana at least once a month, and one out of five smokes cigarettes daily. Children who begin to use drugs before age 15 are *twice as likely* to develop problems with drugs than are children who wait until they are older. Waiting until age 19 to try alcohol or other drugs dramatically decreases the risk of drug problems.

Why is early drug use potentially harmful? Some people can try drugs, use them in moderation, and take them or leave them. Others, however, find that they can't control their use of drugs. No one can tell in advance which people fall

into which group, so everyone takes a risk. In addition, children's bodies are still developing. Their livers are less able to handle alcohol, and they seem to become dependent on chemical substances faster than adults do. Finally, children's bodies are generally *smaller* than adults'. Two cans of beer will have more effect on a 100-pound child than on a 150-pound adult.

Reducing the Risks of Drug Abuse Through Family Bonding

Let's be positive: You *can* do something about your child's chances of getting into trouble with drugs. This isn't just wishful thinking. We said that the more risk factors for drug abuse present, the greater the risk a child will have a problem with drugs. It follows that the fewer risk factors in your family, the *less* risk your child will have a problem with drugs. But how do you reduce the risks?

Let's look at an example: Lynn was only 11 years old, but had already gotten in trouble three times in the past year for vandalism. The last time she had bet a friend that she could throw a rock through the third-story window of an empty

house. She won the bet but got caught, and had to pay for the damage she caused.

Lynn was intelligent but bored. She hung out with a group of children who constantly pressured her to get into trouble, and Lynn often gave in. Both her parents worked during the day and didn't have much time to spend with her, but they loved Lynn and wanted her to live up to her potential: Scolding her for her acts, punishing her by taking away dessert and TV privileges, trying to explain to her why it was wrong to damage property—sometimes these strategies seemed to work, and other times they didn't. Lynn's parents were frustrated.

Then Lynn's mother had an idea.

She asked Lynn if she'd be interested in joining a softball team. When Lynn said sure, why not, Lynn's mother and father took her to a store and let her pick out a new baseball mitt, bat, and softball. They drove her to games and to practice sessions, where the coach taught her how to pitch. They encouraged her progress, and took her out to dinner after she had pitched in her first game.

Meanwhile, Lynn had made friends on the team, and indeed had steadily improved upon her natural skills. When Lynn's old buddies came round, they found that she had better things to do.

What happened? Lynn's parents helped her find a positive alternative to throwing rocks through windows. They included her in the process by helping her decide what equipment she wanted to use. They provided opportunities for her to learn skills which would help her succeed. And they rewarded her when she did succeed. Lynn felt closer to her new friends on the team and to her parents; when that happened she was less susceptible to her old friends' invitations to trouble. Lynn became bonded to her parents: Their actions had made her feel more valuable, more a responsible member of the family.

I t's the same with drugs. You can give your child a positive alternative to drugs, and you can include your child in the process. The key to a positive alternative is building and maintaining strong family relationships. Children with strong family relationships value their parents and sisters and brothers. They feel close to them. They like them. They are "bonded" to their families.

A substantial body of research indicates that children are less likely to get into trouble with drugs if they're bonded to their families—if they feel attached to their parents and sisters and brothers, if they're committed to the family and its values. Family bonds are strengthened when children are involved with their families, when they perform successfully in their families, and when they're rewarded for doing well. Chances are you already do some of these things. We'll help you do more by giving you some information and a few skills to strengthen the bonds in your family, and we'll suggest activities that your whole family can do together. When you work together with your child to strengthen the bonds in your family, you reduce the risk of your child's getting into trouble with drugs. Remember what we said earlier about this book's being like a tool, though: You've got to pick it up and *use* it.

When children are bonded to their family, they're less likely to be influenced by friends who use drugs, and they're less likely to try drugs at an early age, because they don't want to threaten the positive family relationships they've established. When they've learned to make good decisions in the family, they're better able to make good decisions about other important issues they'll be facing as they grow older.

o you remember the 11 factors we listed which increase the risk of drug abuse? Now we want to share with you the three factors we mentioned earlier which *decrease* the risk of drug abuse by strengthening the bonds in your family:

▶ giving your child opportunities to become involved with the family
▶ teaching your child the skills to become involved
▶ rewarding your child for becoming involved

Let's take a closer look at these factors:

1 Giving your child opportunities to become involved with the family. There are many ways for children to become involved in their family, and

any years ago, in a time of dragons and wizards, lived a boy named George. George was barely a teenager, and his energy was boundless. He was always getting into jousts with knaves, and more than once had come under the stern gaze of the ranking lords. His last offense had been the most serious: He had caught a lizard crawling near a neighborhood moat, chopped off its head, and delivered the head to one of the local maidens, frightening her so badly that she swooned.

George fraternized with a group of young ruffians who constantly pressured him to get into trouble, and he often gave in. Both of George's parents tilled the fields during the day and didn't have much time to spend with him, but they loved George and wanted him to live up to his potential. Scolding him for his acts, punishing him by keeping him in the stocks for a few hours, trying to explain to him why it was wrong to kill animals and scare maidens—sometimes these strategies seemed to work, but just as often they didn't. George's parents were frustrated. "Egad!" they often cried, and "Zounds!"

Then George's father had an idea.

After sitting down with his son and asking him what he enjoyed doing the most, George's father asked George if he would be interested in slaying dragons. When George said "Verily, I accept," or words to that effect, George's father and mother took him to a local forgery, where George forged his own sword. They enrolled him in a dragonmaster seminar, where he learned how to wield his sword and feint and avoid dangerous nostril flames. George's parents encouraged his progress, and bought him a shiny helmet with his name engraved in it after he had slain his first small dragon. Meanwhile, George had made friends in the seminar, and indeed had steadily improved upon his natural skills. He had moderated his rowdy behaviors to the extent that some considered him saintly. When George's old ruffians came around, they found that he was in line for knighthood and had little time for them.

What happened? George's parents helped him find a positive alternative to scaring maidens with lizard heads. They included him in the process by helping him decide what equipment he wanted to use. They provided opportunities for him to learn skills which would help him succeed. And they rewarded him when he did succeed. George felt close to his new friends and to his parents; when that happened he was no longer susceptible to his old friends' invitations to trouble.

"(Children who are) not bonded to their school, to their family, or to any other positive social institution . . . are more susceptible to the influence of drug-using peers."

we'll discuss these throughout this book, particularly in the chapter on expanding family roles. Young children may be given a small chore like feeding the cat or setting the table. Older children may take part in some family decisions, like collecting consumer information before the family makes a major purchase. The important thing is for your child to feel like a responsible and significant contributor to the family.

2 Teaching your child how to become involved. Let's take the examples we just mentioned. You may have to show your child where to find the cat food, how much food to put in the dish, and how to call the cat in to eat. And you may have to explain which magazines feature the most reliable consumer information and which kinds of information are helpful in each situation. Your child needs to learn the skills to perform *successfully* in the family. That way everyone benefits.

3 Rewarding your child for becoming involved. You know that *you* like to be recognized for a good job at work, making a special dinner, helping with a community

project, or contributing to any other enterprise. You want your contribution to be noticed and appreciated; it gives you more incentive for continuing to contribute. Children are no different. If you reward them for their successful contributions to the family, then they'll put more energy *into* the family.

We're not necessarily talking about monetary rewards: You don't have to pay your child every time the cat is fed. One of the most powerful rewards anyone can receive is to feel loved. Showing your child your love, *telling* your child "I love you," and repeating it in as many different ways as you can think of is worth more than any denomination of money. There are many ways you can show your love:

▶ giving your child a pat on the back
▶ letting your child hear you tell someone else about how proud you are of your child
▶ taking an interest in your child's activities
▶ sharing stories about your experiences
▶ expressing care when your child isn't feeling well
▶ asking your child for advice

▶ letting your child know that you enjoy the times you spend together
▶ making a special dinner when your child has put out lots of effort

There are also several ways you can tell your child "I love you":

expressing your love in general—
▶ "I'm really lucky to have a (daughter) (son) like you."
▶ "I was thinking today about what a great (daughter) (son) you are."
▶ "I love you."

complimenting specific behaviors—
▶ "I enjoyed _____ with you."
▶ "I feel happy when you _____."
▶ "I'm so proud of the way you _____."

Complimenting specific behaviors not only conveys your love to your child, but it also reinforces those behaviors, making it more likely that your child will continue them.

We'd like you to focus on doing these things, because we believe that expressing your love to your

child is one of the most important things you can do to strengthen the bonds in your family. Begin *now*. It doesn't get any easier to express love, or to have it received, when your child grows into an adolescent.

Throughout this book we'll show you how to involve your child in family activities. We'll teach you some skills that you in turn can teach your child. And we'll show you different ways to reward your child. We think the best way to begin doing all these things, to start preparing for the drug-free years, is to hold family meetings.

Family Meetings "All right, 7:35 p.m., December 13, 1987, the Sludgers family meeting will come to order. Roll call. Sally Sludgers, present. Sidney Sludgers?" "Present." "Susie Sludgers?" "Here." "Sammy Sludgers?" "Yo, Mom." "Baby Sophie Sludgers? Baby Sophie Sludgers!" "Goo." "Fine, all accounted for. First order of business: report on chores for the week ending December 11. Chairman of Chores Committee, I have your written report before me. Would you care to read . . ."

No, that's *not* what we mean by holding a family meeting. Family meetings are a time for *fun*, for *sharing*: What activity can you enjoy together? What's been happening with each family member? How is the family doing as a whole? Is there any news, any event coming up which might interest the family? If you don't like the word "meeting" because it sounds like work, then call it something else—"The Family Sharing Hour," "The Family Get-Together," or just plain "Family Time." This is the time you spend with the people you live with and love in order to make your relationships stronger and closer. This is a time to *look forward to*.

Holding family meetings addresses the following risk factors:

family management, by providing opportunities for your child to be aware of family expectations and the rewards for meeting them and the punishments for not meeting them

alienation, rebelliousness, and lack of social bonding, by helping your child stay involved as a meaningful part of the family

favorable attitudes toward drug use, by giving your child accurate information about drugs, as well as teaching your child skills to examine and reject inaccurate information about drugs

Family meetings provide opportunities for all family members to get involved—in making family decisions, in talking about a sensitive topic, in planning a family celebration, in working out a plan for chores. We recommend holding family meetings once a week for about 45 minutes. Start off easy: Let the purpose of the first family meeting be to plan a fun activity for the whole family. Planning something fun together is not only a great way to practice holding meetings; it's also ideal for encouraging your child's involvement in the family.

What kinds of things are fun for your family?

▶ a dinner at a new ethnic restaurant?
▶ a Sunday drive?
▶ a barbecue?
▶ a party to celebrate a family member's birthday or accomplishment?
▶ a trip to a museum?

▶ a short hike?
▶ a game of cards?
▶ a picnic?
▶ a trip to a library on which everyone gets a book out they think someone else will like?
▶ a jigsaw puzzle the whole family works on?
▶ a visit to a relative in another city?
▶ a sundae-making party?
▶ a trip to a zoo or aquarium?
▶ a picture-taking session for which everyone dresses up?
▶ a camping trip?
▶ a dinner for which everyone cooks one course?
▶ a family garden work party?
▶ a look through the family photograph album?
▶ a neighborhood baseball game?
▶ a cooperative washing of the family car to go to a drive-in movie?

Turn to the agenda for your first family meeting, immediately following this section. On page 18, you'll see spaces for you to put down your own ideas of fun things for your family to do. Take a few minutes now and fill in the spaces with 10 ideas; you can refer to these ideas at your family meeting, when you're

explaining to your family what kind of event you want to plan.

L et's go over some ideas for holding family meetings in general. We'll incorporate these ideas into each family meeting agenda in the book.

Be sure you won't be interrupted.
Everyone needs to agree on a time and place to meet. That may mean that someone has to reschedule a visit with a friend, or do homework earlier, or miss a TV show. If someone has to be inconvenienced, try to come up with a time that doesn't inconvenience the same person each week. Agree not to be interrupted for 45 minutes. That may mean either disconnecting the telephone or asking a family member to take messages until the meeting is over.

Share what will happen in the meeting, and why you think it's important.
Some of the activities in this book are skills you'll be teaching to your family, like how to say no to a friend who's trying to get you to do something that might mean trouble. If family members

learn these skills, then they'll reduce their risk of drug abuse. The other activities, like forming a family policy on drug use and expanding family roles, relate directly to reducing the risks of teenage drug abuse. We suggest telling your family at the beginning of the meeting what the activity's about, and explaining why it will help make the family stronger. If your family knows *why* they're doing what they're doing, then they'll have more reason to participate in the activities.

If you've never held family meetings before, you'll also need to explain why you're holding meetings at all. For this first meeting, that shouldn't be too difficult, because you'll be planning a fun event. At the first meeting you can discuss this book and why you think it's important to hold family meetings. You can tell your family that this is a special time for all of you to be together. You're all working to strengthen the bonds in your family and learn new skills so that your children will feel like an important part of your family and protect themselves from getting in trouble with drugs.

Review the ground rules.
Remember what we said about involvement, and why it's so important for children to feel that they can contribute? The family meeting is not just another time for children to receive orders; they must feel that they have an opportunity to contribute meaningfully to the meeting. Set some ground rules beforehand which will make it easier for *all* of you to have happy and productive discussions. Here are some ground rules which families have found useful:

► Everyone gets a chance to talk.
► One person talks at a time and doesn't get interrupted.
► It's okay to say what you feel.
► No one **has** to talk.
► Everyone has to listen.
► No one puts down anyone else.

You may want to ask family members to suggest other ground rules.

(Use the Familygram, "Ground Rules," at the end of this chapter.)

When you've finished the meeting, review what you've done and set a time for the next meeting.
It's a good idea to review what you've done at the end of a family meeting. This helps ensure that everyone comes away with the same understanding, and it also gives everyone a sense of accomplishment. The end of the meeting is a good time to discuss how to improve future meetings, too. Set a time and place for the next meeting. Some families like to meet at the same time and place each week; others like to vary. See what works best for you.

End the meeting with a game or refreshments.
You may want to rotate the responsibility for coming up with ideas for a short closing game or refreshments, or both. Making it a surprise adds to the fun.

"What if my child thinks that family meetings are a terrible idea and refuses to attend?"
Families handle resistance from their children in different ways. Trying to compel your child to attend the meetings may not be as effective as other ways: It's important for your child to attend the meetings, but it's more important for your child to attend *willingly*. Here are a few ideas:

► **Give your child an incentive** for coming to the meeting. Maybe you can order a pizza afterwards, or do something else your child likes to do.
► **Negotiate with your child:** "If you try this, then I'll try that." Is there something your child has been wanting you to do? Maybe you can trade that for attendance at the meeting.
► **Provide your child with a role** at the meeting, perhaps taking notes or reading the ground rules or helping choose the refreshment. Your child will feel special and a significant part of the meeting.
► **Ask your child to do it as a favor to you.** Explain that everyone's attendance at the meeting is necessary because the meeting is for the good of the family, and the family is very important to you.
► **Say that you need your child there.** Emphasize how much you need your child to contribute to the meeting. After all, one of the main purposes of family meetings is to involve your child in family decisions and activities.
► **Explain the benefits to your child.** Point out that your child is the one who reaps most of the benefits from the family meetings: better protection against drugs; more fun with the family; opportunities to take on greater responsibilities and learn new skills; and receiving more support and rewards from family members. There are many more reasons to attend the meetings than to stay away from them.

So, look over the agenda which follows. We've laid it out so that you can glance at it now and then while you're running the meeting. Don't worry about feeling awkward at first; anything new and worthwhile takes practice. Good luck!

In this chapter, "Getting Started," you've read about how to prevent drug abuse in your family. Now you'll hold a family meeting to discuss family meetings and plan a fun occasion with your family.

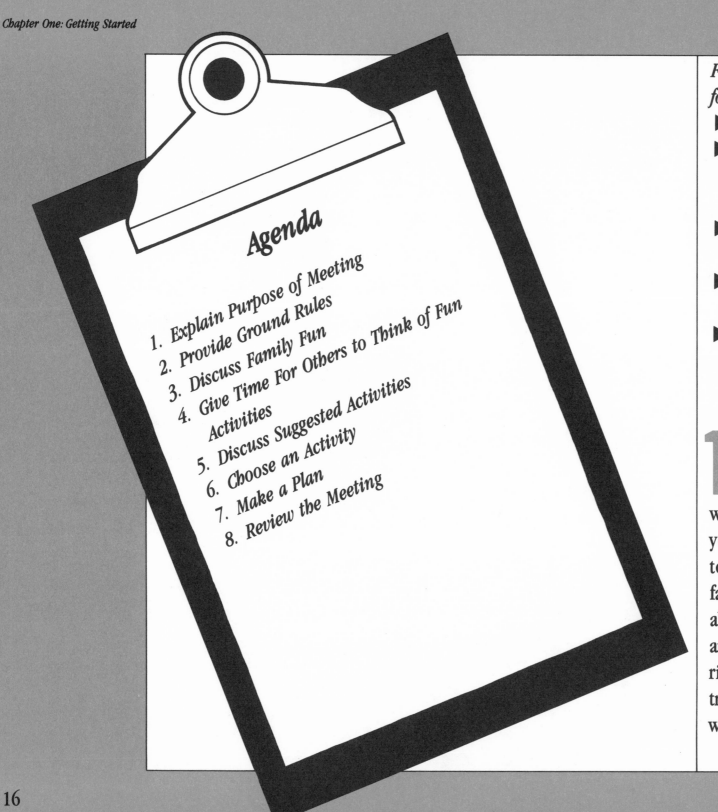

Agenda

1. Explain Purpose of Meeting
2. Provide Ground Rules
3. Discuss Family Fun
4. Give Time For Others to Think of Fun Activities
5. Discuss Suggested Activities
6. Choose an Activity
7. Make a Plan
8. Review the Meeting

For this meeting you'll need the following:

▶ *Familygram, "Ground Rules"*

▶ *your suggestions for fun activities filled out on page 18*

▶ *paper and pencil for each family member*

▶ *Familygram, "Fun Things For the Family To Do"*

▶ *Familygram, "Family Time Is Fun Time!"*

1 Explain Purpose of Meeting

Ask for someone to take phone messages so that the meeting won't be interrupted. Say that you're glad everyone could come to the meeting. Explain to your family that you're concerned about drug abuse among children, and that you want to reduce the risk of your child's getting into trouble with drugs. Point out three ways you'll be trying to do that:

- giving your child opportunities to become involved in the family
- teaching your child how to become involved
- rewarding your child for becoming involved

Briefly describe this book. Explain that the book suggests holding regular family meetings as a way to make the family stronger, closer, and happier, and in that way to strengthen the bonds in your family.

2 Provide Ground Rules
Provide ground rules for this and future meetings. Let everyone get a chance to comment and make suggestions. Display the ground rules where everyone can see them during the meeting.

(Use the Familygram, "Ground Rules," at the end of this chapter.)

3 Discuss Family Fun
Tell everyone that the purpose of this meeting is to plan something fun for the family to do together. Talk about some of the fun times you've had together in the past—use photographs if you have any—and say that you'd like to have more of those times. Share the suggestions from the next page that you wrote down earlier:

Ground Rules

- Everyone gets a chance to talk.

- One person talks at a time and doesn't get interrupted.

- It's okay to say what you feel.

- No one **has** to talk.

- Everyone has to listen.

- No one puts down anyone else.

Family Fun

_____

_____

_____

_____

_____

_____

_____

_____

4 Give Time For Others To Think of Fun Activities

Give everyone a few minutes to think of their own ideas. Give sheets of paper and pencils to anyone who wants to write down their ideas. You may want to set some restrictions beforehand, for example, time and cost.

5 Discuss Suggested Activities

Write down people's suggestions on the Familygram, "Fun Things For the Family To Do," which you can find at the end of this chapter. Let everyone make suggestions, *without any criticism*. After everyone has run out of ideas, review the suggestions, asking the group for the advantages and disadvantages of each.

6 Choose an Activity

Choose at least one activity. One way to do this is to ask all family members to vote for three activities not their own. Some families like to use different-colored stickers for this purpose. If there's a tie, have another vote, or do both activities, flipping a coin to decide which to do first. You may want to do all the activities eventually, alternating, for example, activities done away from home with those done at home.

7 Make a Plan

Make a commitment to follow through with the activity chosen by beginning to set up a specific plan, for example, selecting a date and time and displaying a notice where everyone can see it. You can write down some of this information on the

Familygram, "Fun Things For the Family To Do."

Try to do the activity within a week or two. You can divide the tasks so that everyone gets a chance to be involved. For example, if you're going to visit a museum, your child could call ahead to check out the visiting hours and cost of admission. Make sure everyone knows where you'll be displaying information about the activity.

8 Review the Meeting

Review what you've done in this meeting, and ask if anyone has any ideas how to make the next meeting even better. Set a time for the next meeting, select a person to be in charge of the next meeting's game or refreshments, and end with *your* game or refreshments. Display the Familygram, "Family Time Is **Fun** Time!"

FAMILY
TIME
IS
FUN
TIME!

Other Activities for *Getting Started*

Use these activities as further opportunities for your children to become involved with the family, to learn new skills, and to be rewarded for participating.

1. Something Special

In the week before the meeting, ask each family member to think of something of special personal interest or meaning—e.g., a newspaper clipping, a photograph, an object—and bring it to the meeting. At the end of the meeting, each person gets a chance to talk about "something special." This activity provides the opportunity not only for sharing, but also for validating your child's feelings about something personally meaningful.

A variation of this activity is for family members to think of the best thing that happened to them during the past week. This gives everyone another chance to feel good about a recent event.

2. The Family Album

Bring a family album, maybe of parents' and grandparents' childhood photographs, to the meeting. After your child chooses photographs, you can talk about what the people in them were doing and what the family was like at that time. Be prepared to share some interesting anecdotes, particularly about skills your relatives had or the way they lived. "The Family Album" lends a sense of continuity to your family, a sense of pride, and perhaps incentive for your child to become an integral part of it.

3. Parents as Children

Children are usually very interested in what their parents were like when *they* were children. You can share parts of your earlier life with your child by recalling events of years ago, for example:

► why your favorite teacher was important to you
► your first date
► ways you contributed to your family
► a good time you had with your best friend
► what you did for entertainment
► a time you got in trouble

Letting your child into your life lets your child feel more attached to you and as a result more bonded to the family.

4. Big Questions

Family members take turns answering any or all of the following questions:

► What is the nicest thing anyone has done for you?
► Who is the person outside the family you admire most?

▶ What is the most difficult thing in life for you now?

▶ What have you done that you're most proud of?

You may want to add other big questions to the list. Sharing personal information is an effective way of strengthening the bonds between a group of people.

5. The Family Olympics

Have a friendly competition within your own family! Let each family member choose one or more events in which everyone must compete. The events can be physical or mental. Here are some examples:

▶ skipping rope
▶ saying a tongue-twister
▶ naming animals beginning with each letter of the alphabet
▶ balancing a stack of pennies
▶ memorizing a series of numbers
▶ playing croquet

You can set aside an afternoon for the events, or space them out over a period of a week or more. Decide on a system for scoring, and award prizes at the end of the tournament.

6. Jar of Fun

Place in a jar note cards of fun things for your family to do, and pick a note card from the jar whenever you have some time together. You may want to use different-colored note cards for outside activities and inside activities, or activities which cost a little money and activities which cost nothing, etc.. Replenish the jar with new activities, so that the jar is always full.

"... Children are usually very interested in what their parents were like when *they* were children. You can share parts of your earlier life with your child by recalling events of years ago ..."

Ground Rules

1. Everyone gets a chance to talk.

2. One person talks at a time and doesn't get interrupted.

3. It's okay to say what you feel.

4. No one *has* to talk.

5. Everyone has to listen.

6. No one puts down anyone else.

7. _____

8. _____

9. _____

10. _____

Fun Things for the Family to Do

1. _____
2. _____
3. _____
4. _____
5. _____
6. _____
7. _____
8. _____
9. _____
10. _____
11. _____
12. _____
13. _____
14. _____
15. _____
16. _____
17. _____
18. _____
19. _____
20. _____
21. _____
22. _____
23. _____
24. _____
25. _____
26. _____
27. _____
28. _____
29. _____
30. _____

The Plan

The Activity: _____

The Date: _____

The Time: _____

The Details: _____

Family GRAM

FAMILY TIME IS *FUN* TIME!

Chapter Two
Setting Guidelines:
How to Develop a Family Position on Drugs

What do you want for your child? Picture all your hopes and dreams for your child coming true, a vision of the future in which everything that you wish for your child happens. What does that vision look like?

Now consider the following questions:

▶ How do you feel about your child's having a beer now and then?

▶ What would you do if you found cigarette papers in your child's bedroom?

▶ Do you expect your child to stay away from all drugs throughout junior high and high school?

▶ Does your child know your family's rules for drug use?

▶ Is beer considered a drug in your home?

▶ Is it okay for your child to have a glass of champagne at a wedding?

▶ Are there any rules for *your* use of drugs?

Were you able to answer all of those questions? Have you thought about them before? You're aware of the harmful effects of drug abuse, and now you have some idea of the factors which increase the risk of your child's getting into trouble with drugs. But how can

you translate that awareness into practical guidelines for your family? And having done that, how do you persuade your child to follow the guidelines?

In this chapter we'll help you address some of these questions. You'll share your vision with your child, and you'll base your expectations of family members' drug use on trying to make that vision a reality. That's the point: Your hopes and dreams for your child are reason enough to agree on a position which reduces the risks of getting into trouble with drugs.

Developing a family position on drugs addresses the following risk factors:

family management, by providing opportunities for your child to participate in setting family expectations regarding drug use, as well as the rewards for meeting those expectations and the punishments for not meeting them

parental drug use and positive parental attitudes toward use, by sharing your feelings about the use of drugs with your child

favorable attitudes toward

drug use, by teaching your child the reasons to avoid getting into trouble with drugs

early first use of drugs, by teaching your child the consequences of early drug use

The process has five steps:

▶ **Step #1.**
Clarify a vision for your child.

▶ **Step #2.**
Decide what specific behaviors you expect concerning the use of drugs.

▶ **Step #3.**
Determine with your family a position on drugs.

▶ **Step #4.**
List the consequences of following and of not following the guidelines.

▶ **Step #5.**
Review the family position regularly.

Let's take a look at this process one step at a time. You can teach it to your family at the next family meeting.

Step #1
Clarify a vision for your child.

When you're clear about what you'd like for your child, then you can provide good reasons for the positions you take on drugs, both to yourself and your child. Your drug position becomes more than just a list of rules; it becomes a road map showing the direction you want your child to move in. The emphasis shifts from "don't" to "do."

What do parents wish for their children? Some wishes may be very specific—"get good grades and graduate from high school." Some of them may be more general—"recognize your accomplishments and feel good about them." Here are some other wishes for children:

▶ Be happy.
▶ Be able to make good decisions.
▶ Be healthy.
▶ Be a responsible citizen.
▶ Treat yourself and others with respect.
▶ Make the most of your strengths.

Notice that all of these wishes are positive. They're not "Don't ever . . ." or "Stay away from . . ." This is important; children need to know that their parents want to help their children become the best they can, that this is the source of your concern about drugs.

Take a look at the agenda for the family meeting in the next section. On page 37 write down at least three wishes to share with your child at the next family meeting. If you have more than one child, the vision may be the same *or* different for each one. At the family meeting, you'll fill out a Familygram, "Wishes for _____," which you can find at the end of this chapter. You can begin this Familygram by writing down some things you *like* about your child. There's also space for your child to write a personal vision, since your child's vision may differ from your own.

Step #2
Decide what specific behaviors you expect concerning the use of drugs.

Given what you know about the risk factors for drug abuse, how might the potential of the wishes you've just written for your child be affected if your child used drugs? For example, if you have a dream of your child enjoying robust health, what are your expectations concerning your child's use of tobacco? If you wish that your child will get good grades in school, what are your

expectations concerning your child's use of marijuana?

Think about how drugs might affect your child:

▶ financially—spending money on drugs or on fines for driving under the influence; having a hard time making money because of getting fired from jobs
▶ legally—having a record because of stealing to get money to pay for drugs, or because of hurting someone while under the influence of drugs
▶ physically—not having enough breath to play most sports because of smoking; not having enough coordination to do any delicate work because of drinking; not having enough concentration to do intellectual work because of using marijuana.
▶ emotionally—not having many good friends because of abusing drugs: No one can really depend on someone with a drug habit, because the drug can become more important than the other person; not being able to start a family, because of not being trusted

Think carefully about your expectations, not only concerning different drugs, but also concerning different situations, like the following:

▶ trying marijuana
▶ drinking wine at a family dinner
▶ going to parties where drinks are served
▶ reading drug-related magazines
▶ riding in a car with people who have been drinking or using other drugs

Writing down your expectations and thinking about *specific behaviors* will eventually produce a clearer position. The specific guidelines will also be easier for your child to remember, especially when pressured by others to use drugs. "I expect that you will stay away from drugs" is not an effective guideline if your child doesn't consider alcohol a drug, or feels free to bring drug paraphernalia into the house, or doesn't mind riding in a car with people who are under the influence of drugs. Effective guidelines are specific and cover situations in which family members are likely to find themselves. Try to limit your guidelines to those situations, however; it's not wise to have

Developing a Family Position on Drugs

1. Clarify a vision for your child.
2. Decide what specific behaviors you expect concerning the use of drugs.
3. Determine with your family a position on drugs.
4. List the consequences of following and of not following the guidelines.
5. Review the family position regularly.

"In order to make good decisions about their behavior, children need to get from their family clear guidelines for acceptable and unacceptable behavior."

so many rules that they aren't taken seriously.

Here are a few examples of specific expectations:

▶ You will not use nicotine in any form, for example, cigarettes, cigars, pipe tobacco, or chewing tobacco.

▶ You will not drink any alcoholic beverages, for example, beer, wine, hard liquor, or drinks made with wine or liquor.

▶ You will not accept a ride with anyone who appears to be or actually is under the influence of a drug, but will instead stay where you are and call home for a ride.

N ow take a look at the agenda for the next family meeting. On page 39 write down several of your expectations about your child and drug use. These will form the basis for your discussions at the meeting. Children as well as adults are more likely to respect and follow rules if they understand the reasoning behind them, so when you're writing your expectations, consider *why* you're writing them. *Developing a position on drugs works only if the entire family understands the*

rules and if you're fair and consistent in enforcing them.

Step #3
Determine with your family a position on drugs.

When you hold your family meeting, discuss your vision for your child, and then compare it with your child's own vision. Talk about how the use of drugs affects that vision. Review each of your expectations, along with your reasoning for each, let each family member voice an opinion, and change your expectations as appropriate. Your child should feel like a significant participant in this discussion. Involving your child in the discussion not only helps to strengthen bonding, but it also enables your child to feel more committed to the position your family eventually adopts. Although you'll be following ground rules, and everyone's opinion will be heard, you will obviously have the final say on expected behaviors. Consider using the following guidelines for family discussions:

▶ Ask other family members for their opinions.

▶ Listen attentively, looking at each speaker.

▶ If necessary, restate what someone has said to make sure that you've understood both the content and the feelings of whoever's speaking.

▶ Emphasize the points on which everyone agrees, and try to work out the points on which people disagree.

▶ Reach a decision, keeping in mind that you have the final responsibility for the family and thus the final decision.

▶ Make sure that everyone understands the decision and its implications.

Step #4
List the consequences of following and of not following the guidelines.

D eveloping a family position on drugs wouldn't mean much if you didn't enforce it. What happens if you discover that your child was smoking cigarettes after school? What happens if your child comes home and confesses it? On the other hand, what happens if your child goes through the first year of junior high school without once using drugs? Consequences can be positive as well as negative: Be at least as ready to reward as to punish.

Listing consequences of following and of not following the behaviors you expect from your child, and enforcing those consequences, lets your child know that you're serious about the family position. Be prepared to do what you say you'll do: Will you really ground your child for a month because your child smoked a cigarette? Will you really buy your child a TV for staying away from drugs for a year?

A re the consequences realistic and appropriate? Harsh punishment indicates a major violation of the guidelines; barely acknowledging the behavior gives the opposite impression.

Here are a few positive consequences you might consider for rewarding your child:

▶ doing your child a special favor

▶ buying tickets to a sporting event

▶ having friends over for pizza

▶ choosing the menu for a week

And here are a few negative consequences:

▶ no allowance

- no use of telephone, TV, or video
- extra chores
- no visits with friends

It's especially important that negative consequences follow the violation of a guideline as soon as possible. Similarly, positive consequences should not be delayed too long, or the connection between the act and the consequences will be weakened. Again, look at your family agenda, and on page 39 list some positive and some negative consequences for the expectations you listed before. Discuss consequences as you did expectations, and reach a decision.

At this family meeting, then, you'll be discussing three things:
- a vision for your child
- the specific behaviors expected from your child concerning the use of drugs
- the consequences of following and of not following those behaviors

When everyone is clear about the vision, the expected behaviors, and the positive and negative consequences, display the family position where everyone can see it and not

forget it. Using the previous examples, it could look something like the examples to the right.

(Use the Familygram, "Our Family Position on Drugs" at the end of this chapter.)

Displaying the position not only helps validate everyone's contribution, but it also provides a visual reminder that your child can point to if pressured by a friend to violate the guidelines.

Step #5.
Review the family position regularly.

Circumstances change. As your child grows older, you may want to reconsider some of the items in your agreement. Maybe your child is developing new interests, which in turn may alter the vision. Or you may find that as new situations arise—getting a driver's license, going to parties—you need to change your expectations. And the specific rewards and punishments you've listed for a fourth-grader may no longer be appropriate for a seventh-grader. It's a good idea to set a time—for example, at the end of the school year—to review

the family position and make any necessary changes.

Let's try to answer some questions you may have about this activity:

"Won't forming a position on drug use just put ideas in my child's head?"
As we've said, most children have already been exposed to nicotine, alcohol, and marijuana by the time they leave junior high school. It's doubtful that you're giving your child any *new* ideas. What we hope is that, by relating drug use to the vision for your child, by stating clear consequences for your child's actions, and by involving your child in the process, you'll be giving your child *positive* ideas, and reasons to avoid drugs before a friend offers them.

"I occasionally drink myself. Is it fair to have different expectations for my child?"
It's fair if you explain why drinking is a greater risk for a child than for an adult. Drugs have more serious effects on minds and bodies that are still physiologically developing, and the research clearly points out how dangerous it is for children to use drugs before age 15. In addition, it's illegal for children to use alcohol and other drugs.

What We Expect:
You will not drink any alcoholic beverages, for example, beer, wine, hard liquor, or drinks made with wine or liquor.

Consequences of Meeting Expectation:
after three months, choosing the menu for a week

Consequences of Not Meeting Expectation:
extra chores

What We Expect:
You will not use nicotine in any form, for example, cigarettes, cigars, pipe tobacco, or chewing tobacco.

Consequences of Meeting Expectation:
after three months, having friends over for pizza

Consequences of Not Meeting Expectation:
no allowance for a month

What We Expect:
You will not accept a ride with anyone who appears to be or actually is under the influence of a drug, but will instead stay where you are and call home for a ride.

Consequences of Meeting Expectation:
after six months, tickets to a sporting event

Consequences of Not Meeting Expectation:
no visits with friends for 3 weeks, no parties for 3 months

Unbelievable Tales in Family Drug Prevention:
The Stonecutter's Legacy

 n 356 B.C. the family of Yen-tsi, living in rural northern China, set the record for most visions in a family with 38. A stonecutter and day laborer, Yen-tsi insisted that his wife and three sons spend their evenings setting guidelines for using wild roots and herbs as well as driving the yak to unchaperoned parties. The Yen-tsis were a patient family, and it took them two years alone just to sort through the visions and begin to discuss expectations. While they talked, they worked, since their family motto was "No tongue is long enough to bind the hand." Slowly they began to cut stones and fit them together into a barrier in their backyard, talking and working, talking and working.

Several weeks later at a block party Yen-tsi told his neighbor about setting family guidelines and working with his hands as a way to stimulate thought. The neighbor thought this an excellent idea, and began to set guidelines with his family. They, too, began to work as they talked.

 oon the whole countryside was talking and working. In the year 342 someone had the idea of connecting their little walls together into one great wall. Yen-tsi's family was stuck on determining consequences for a year and a half, but finally displayed their family position on the wall seventeen years later, after The Great Brainstorm of 326. People continued building the wall and setting guidelines, until the year 215, when the wall extended 1400 miles, and displayed over 350 family positions. Yen-tsi had died more than a century earlier, but his original family position was enshrined on The Great Wall in a rather lovely ceremony.

There are other behaviors besides using alcohol—for example, driving a car—that society reserves for adults.

"What happens when my child grows up and leaves home? Shouldn't I allow my child to drink now, under my supervision?"
Many families feel that even supervised drinking in the teen years is not worth the increased risk of drug abuse later. Clearly, your child is at increased risk by drinking before age 15, even under your supervision.

"Is there a way to bring up the topic of drugs before the family meeting?"
You may find that it's a good time to comment on the effects of drugs when you see a beer commercial on TV, or when you read about a drinking/driving accident in the newspaper. You can point out that some people take drugs to make them feel better about themselves, but that they often don't ever learn how to do that without drugs. You can also say that it's difficult to know at first who will be able to handle drugs and who won't. You can then describe some of the results of drug abuse. Get your family comfortable discussing the issues.

When you feel confident about this section, it will be time to hold your family meeting and develop your position on drugs. In the meantime, you can be writing down your vision and your expectations. Read through the following agenda. As in the last section, we'll take you through the meeting. Be sure to *listen* to what everyone says: It's the whole family's meeting. Good luck!

In this chapter, "Setting Guidelines," you've read about how to develop a family position on drugs. Now you'll hold a family meeting to share the vision you have for your child, the specific behaviors you expect concerning the use of drugs, and the consequences of following and of not following those behaviors. Together your family will develop a position on drug use.

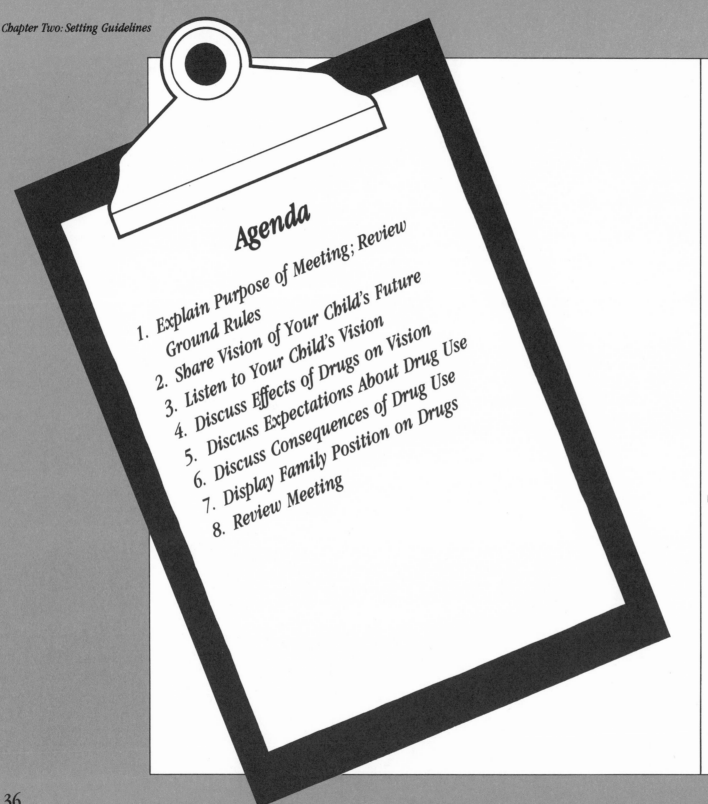

Agenda

1. Explain Purpose of Meeting; Review Ground Rules
2. Share Vision of Your Child's Future
3. Listen to Your Child's Vision
4. Discuss Effects of Drugs on Vision
5. Discuss Expectations About Drug Use
6. Discuss Consequences of Drug Use
7. Display Family Position on Drugs
8. Review Meeting

For this meeting you'll need the following:

▶ *your vision for your child filled out on page 37*

▶ *Familygram, "Wishes for _____"*

▶ *your suggested expectations filled out on page 39*

▶ *Familygram, "Our Family Position on Drugs"*

▶ *your suggested consequences filled out on page 39*

▶ *Familygram, "Everybody's Future Turns Out Better Without Drugs"*

1 Explain Purpose of Meeting; Review Ground Rules

Ask for someone to take phone messages so that the meeting won't be interrupted. Say that you're glad everyone could come to the meeting. Explain that the purpose of this meeting is to develop a family position on drugs, and review the ground rules.

Ground Rules

▶ Everyone gets a chance to talk.

▶ One person talks at a time and doesn't get interrupted.

▶ It's okay to say what you feel.

▶ No one **has** to talk.

▶ Everyone has to listen.

▶ No one puts down anyone else.

▶ _____

▶ _____

▶ _____

2 Share Vision of Your Child's Future

Begin by describing some things you like about your child. Add that you have a vision for your child—hopes and dreams. Explain that you wrote this vision down because you want your child to know how much you care and why you make rules. Read or refer to the vision you wrote earlier.

Your Vision for Your Child

_____

_____

_____

_____

_____

_____

_____

_____

_____

3 Listen to Your Child's Vision

Discuss your child's own views of the vision, and let your child express personal goals. Together fill out the Familygram, "Wishes for _____," which you can find at the end of this chapter.

4 Discuss Effects of Drugs on Vision

Take the time to express how much you care about your child, and discuss how the visions may be harder to achieve if your child becomes involved with drugs. For example:

▶ Smoking may impair your child's health to the extent that participation in sports or music would be difficult.

▶ Use of marijuana would hurt your child's ability to concentrate in school.

▶ Use of alcohol would increase the chances of your child's becoming involved in a serious accident.

On the back side of the Familygram, "Wishes for _____," write down how the particular visions for your child may be affected by drugs. Point out that even though drug use may not be a problem for the family now, it may be an issue in the future, and it's a good idea to be ready for it.

5 Discuss Expectations about Drug Use

Explain the importance of setting down specific behaviors concerning the use of drugs. Share the expectations you've previously written, and give your reasons for each.

Discuss the expectations, one at a time, with your family. Listen attentively to everyone, restating what people said if necessary. Try to close the gaps where family members have differences, and determine the expected behaviors about drug use in your family. Keep in mind that you have the final say on family decisions. Make sure that everyone understands which decisions have been made and what they mean, and begin to fill out the Familygram, "Our Family Position on Drugs."

6 Discuss Consequences of Drug Use

Using the same procedure, determine the positive consequences of following the behaviors and the negative consequences of not following them. Use the consequences you previously wrote down as a basis for discussion.

Expectations
about Drug Use

_____

_____

_____

_____

_____

_____

_____

Consequences
Positive   Negative

7 Display Family Position on Drugs

Complete the Familygram, "Our Family Position on Drugs," and display it in a place where everyone can be reminded of it. You may want to make copies of it for each member of the family. **Keep it visible!**

8 Review Meeting

Review what you've done in this meeting, and ask if anyone has any ideas how to make the next meeting even better. Set a time for the next meeting, select a person to be in charge of the next meeting's game or refreshments, and end with a game or refreshments. Display the Familygram, "Everybody's Future Turns Out Better **Without** Drugs."

1. Getting to Know Me

This activity is a fun way for family members to discuss what is important to each of them. Using a list like the one below—you can add or take away items from the list—ask each member to make a "V" next to those items that are personally very important, "S" next to those items that are somewhat important, and "N" next to those items that are not important:

▶ being the best at school or at work
▶ having time alone
▶ helping at home
▶ eating healthy foods
▶ having a hobby
▶ playing sports
▶ getting exercise
▶ being with friends
▶ wearing nice clothes
▶ watching television
▶ being on time
▶ listening to music
▶ spending time with the family

When all family members are through marking their lists, exchange the lists so that no one knows whose is whose (It's good for everyone to use a pencil or everyone to use the same -colored pen for this to have a chance to work). Then take turns reading the items, guessing who made which marks, and discussing the results. You may be surprised at what you find out about the members of your family.

2. *Baloney!*

This activity can be done while watching TV, riding in a car, or even winding up a family meeting. Advertisements for drugs—particularly nicotine and alcohol—are all around us; many of these advertisements are misleading and sensational. You can make fun of these advertisements by spoofing them—"rewriting" them so that they tell the truth humorously. In this way your family not only makes fun of the ads but also learns to be more aware of the influence of the media or society's use of drugs. When you see or hear an advertisement for drugs (or anything else) that is stretching the truth, yell "Baloney!" Then the whole family can participate in a take-off on the ad. You may also want to look through magazines and then write or draw spoofs at the end of a family meeting.

For example, a commercial on TV may feature a former athlete singing the praises of a particular brand of beer. Your child can yell "Baloney!" and then restage the commercial by pretending to be the athlete: "I used to be an All-Pro defensive lineman. But then I started drinking _____ beer. I started getting fatter and slower. I missed a couple of practices because of hangovers from the night before. I got into a few fights. Then I missed half a season because I broke my arm in a car crash; I was a little drunk at the time. Now I'm retired. All I do is sit around and drink with the rest of the guys who have to make commercials because they're not good enough to play ball anymore."

Other Activities for *Setting Guide-lines*

Use these activities as further opportunities for your children to become involved with the family, to learn new skills, and to be rewarded for participating.

You may want to point out to your child some of the techniques advertisers use to persuade people to buy their products, for example:

▶ *testimonial* — the ad shows important or famous people "testifying" that the product is good, even though they may know nothing about it.

▶ *transfer* — the ad has good-looking or successful people selling the product, implying that if you buy it you will also be good-looking or successful.

▶ *bandwagon* — the ad pretends that everyone is using the product, and that something is wrong with you if you don't, too.

▶ *appeal to the senses* — the ad presents high-tech images and sounds, hoping that you associate the fancy commercial with the quality of the product.

▶ *plain folks* — the ad shows someone "off the street" saying good things about the product, suggesting that that person represents a large majority of people.

When you explain some of these techniques to your child, your child can more easily recognize them when they're used and even use them in the spoofs all of you make up.

3. Space Colony

You're the master planner for a colony of Earthpeople who have just landed on Mars to start a new world. Everyone is looking to you to make the rules for a society which will be happy, healthy, and productive. One of the areas you need to work on is laws concerning drugs. Among the questions you have to consider are:

▶ Should **any** drugs be permitted on Mars?
▶ If no, why not?
▶ If yes, which ones? Why?
▶ Should only certain people be permitted to use them? If yes, which ones?

Questions like these prompt your child to think about both the benefits and the harmfulness of drugs, for example, the taste of wine as opposed to the increased number of motor vehicle accidents. Your family can discuss these issues, and then transfer the issues from the Martian colony to Earth, to your neighborhood, and finally to your family.

4. Heroes

Children usually have heroes—people they look up to and wish to emulate. The hero could be a teacher, a neighbor, or a family friend. Ask to talk about whom your child admires; focus on why these people are admirable, and how their characteristics would change if they used drugs. This activity is an opportunity for you to thank the people your child admires, and to encourage them to continue being healthy role models for your child.

"... Many families have someone who has been in trouble with drugs—an alcoholic, a heavy smoker, etc. ... talk to your child about the history of drugs in your family ..."

5. The Progressive Story

The whole family can make up a story about some of the issues around drug use. Start the story yourself; the main character could be a child the age of your child. For instance, "Lindsay was in the seventh grade, and new to her school. She didn't know anyone, and felt kind of lonely. Then one day after school she was approached by a girl she'd noticed in her math class; the girl asked her if she wanted to go to a party that weekend. As she spoke, the girl took a pack of cigarettes from her purse, lit one of the cigarettes, and offered one to Lindsay." After you set up a situation, someone else can continue the story, and so on. You can make the story funny, or you can make it difficult for the person who speaks after you by getting the main character in a "cliff-hanging" situation. Since everyone will get a chance to speak several times, you'll have opportunities to control the content of the story to some extent. Not only can you give your child important messages about the consequences of using drugs, but you can also see what decisions your child makes to get the characters out of tough situations.

6. Drugs in the Family Tree

Many families have someone who has been in trouble with drugs—an alcoholic, a heavy smoker, etc.. Share some of this information with your child: Talk to your child about the history of drugs in your family. You can do this without criticizing anyone for their drug problems by discussing the subject under the framework of illnesses running in families. If you or your spouse, or the parents of you or your spouse have had problems with alcohol or other drugs, then your child is at an increased risk of drug abuse, and may have to be much more careful about using alcohol or other drugs at all, even as an adult. Sharing personal information "brings the issue home" to children as well; hearing about an uncle who died of smoking-related emphysema is often more meaningful than hearing you merely state that nicotine is a major cause of lung disease.

Wishes for

Date: _____

What I like about _____

_____

_____

My wishes for _____

_____

_____

_____

Signature _____

My wishes for myself: _____

_____

_____

Family GRAM

Our Family Position on Drugs

Date: _____

	What We Expect	Consequences of Meeting Expectation	Consequences of Not Meeting Expectation
1.			
2.			
3.			
4.			
5.			
6.			
7.			
8.			
9.			
10.			

_____
Signature

_____
Signature

_____
Signature

_____
Signature

Family GRAM

EVERYBODY'S FUTURE TURNS OUT BETTER *WITHOUT* DRUGS.

Chapter Three
Avoiding Trouble:
How to Say No to Drugs

Even if you don't drink, try to imagine yourself in this situation: You're at a friend's party, you've had a glass of wine, and you're having a pretty good time talking to people. You don't want to drink any more because you have to drive home soon, and home is 15 miles away. Now one of the louder people at the party you noticed before approaches you with a pitcher of a red liquid, smiles, hiccups, and says to you, "Hey, try some of this special punch! It's great! I mean, it's got all kinds of stuff in it! Rum, vodka, bourbon, who knows, I think there's even some fruit juice in it! **Let me fill your glass!**" What would you do?

Well, you'd probably say something like "No, thanks," or cover your glass with your hand. If the person insisted, you could always just turn the other way or even walk across the room. The situation isn't very pleasant, but it's not too difficult, right?

Okay, same party. You've had some wine, and you know you want to leave soon. This time, however, your good friend Carla, the hostess of the party, approaches you with the pitcher. "Hey," she says to you,

"I've been wanting to make this for ages. I'd really like you to try it. Rum, vodka, bourbon, but it's smooth. *I* think it's the best drink around, but I wouldn't want anyone else to try it before you gave it your official okay. **Let me fill your glass!**"

Things are a little different now, aren't they? In fact, you're a little bit on the spot. You really don't want to drink anymore, but Carla *is* your good friend. Plus, she's the one throwing the party, and it would be rude to refuse. You can't just ignore her and walk away. This *is* a difficult situation. How do you stay out of trouble and not put off Carla? And how can you continue to have fun at the party without drinking the punch?

This is a problem that children face when their friends ask them to get into trouble, whether it's riding with someone under the influence of drugs or cheating on a test or shoplifting. It's not the stranger in a trench coat that gets a child to try a cigarette, or a beer, or a joint, but usually a child's friend or brother or sister who first makes the offer. It's pretty easy to say no to a stranger. It's hard to say no to a friend; when was the last time *you* did it? Your children may want to stay out of trouble, but probably not at the expense of losing their friends and missing out on fun.

We're going to help you teach your family something called *Refusal Skills®*. The goals of *Refusal Skills®* are:

▶ **to keep your friends**
▶ **to have fun**
▶ **to stay out of trouble**

When strangers try to get your children into trouble, your children should say no, get away, and tell someone about it. When "friends" consistently try to get your children into trouble, your children should seriously consider making new friends. *Refusal Skills®* are for people—adults and children—who occasionally find themselves in a tough spot with their friends. We think you'll find this as useful as your children will.

Teaching a Skill
Teaching a skill, like the skill itself, takes practice. You'll be teaching several skills to your child throughout this book, and the process is the same for each skill. So is this advice: **Relax.** Have some fun with the skill. Laugh with your child. You're learning, your child is learning, and you're strengthening the bonds in your family. Be patient with each other, and support each other. You'll find that you're all natural teachers.

We'll briefly repeat these steps for you in the family agenda section. For now, consider the following:

1 **Model the steps one at a time.** Make sure your child or whoever is learning the skill understands and can do the step before going on to the next one. When you get to Step #2, have your child repeat Step #1. When you get to Step #3, have your child repeat Steps #1 and #2, and so on. Act out the steps, and keep verbal explanations to a minimum. Use the examples for the skill we give you, then make up some of your own. Make up realistic examples, so your child can relate to the situation. You may want to "think out loud," so that your child can understand the thought processes behind each step of the skill.

2 **Coach family members who want to learn the skill.** You can help your child or other family members who are trying to learn the skill by giving them the key words when they get stuck. Say exactly what you want your child to repeat. If the key words are "Instead why don't we . . .," don't say "Say 'Instead why don't we . . .'." Say "Instead why don't we . . ." Use the same key words each time, until your child becomes comfortable with the skill.

3 **Give feedback.** Make the feedback constructive. Explain specifically how your child can improve, and offer encouragement. Emphasize that everyone finds learning new skills difficult. Here's an example: "You did really well that time! Let's try it again, but this time look right into my eyes when you talk."

4 **Practice.** Keep practice sessions short, and vary the situations. Practice the skill in situations where your child is likely to use it—at the store, walking to school, on the playground—and encourage your child to practice it with friends.

5 **Reward your child.** Some parents like to present their children with homemade "Certificates of Achievement" for learning a skill. Think of an appropriate reward to show that you're proud your child mastered the skill.

6 **Have fun!** Use props if you want. Laugh with your child. Throw in a silly example. If you get tense, then your child will probably get tense, and learning will be much more difficult.

Now let's discuss *Refusal Skills®*.

Refusal Skills®
Using *Refusal Skills®* addresses the following risk factors:
antisocial behavior in early adolescence, by teaching your child how to avoid trouble
friends who use drugs, by teaching your child how to resist pressure from friends to try drugs
early first use of drugs, by teaching your child how to stay away from drugs at a time of significant risk

The process has five steps:

"Even children who grow up without other risk factors but who associate with children who use drugs are at an increased risk for developing problems with drugs."

Refusal Skills®

1. Ask questions.
2. Name the trouble.
3. Identify the consequences.
4. Suggest an alternative.
5. Move it, sell it, and leave the door open.

▶ **Step #1.**
Ask questions.
▶ **Step #2.**
Name the trouble.
▶ **Step #3.**
Identify the consequences.
▶ **Step #4.**
Suggest an alternative.
▶ **Step #5.**
Move it, sell it, and leave the door open.

Each step has a few KEY WORDS you say to the person who's trying to get you in trouble. The key words help you remember what to say for each step of the skill. Let's take one step at a time.

Remember Carla, trying to get you to drink the punch? The situation could apply to your child as well, but first we'll see how *you* might use the skill.

Step #1
Ask questions.
(Key words—any words like "What . . ." or "Why . . ." which begin questions that get at the possibility of trouble, for example, "What are we going to do there?" or "Why do you want me to do that?")

Carla: *"Hey, I've been wanting to make this for ages. I'd really like you to try it."*
You: *"What's in it?"*

Carla: *"Rum, vodka, bourbon, but it's smooth."*

At this point, the first step is over. You can stop asking questions, because now you have enough information to know that you want to say no. You don't have to ask Carla what kind of rum is in the drink; you don't have to ask her how smooth it is. The first step is to ask questions until you know there's trouble.

Children get asked to do a lot of things which might be trouble. Often, however, they need to ask their friends a question or two to find out if it really *is* trouble. The most common question children need to ask is *"What are we going to do?"*

"Let's meet in the parking lot after school."
"What are we going to do?"
"We're going to put shaving cream all over Mr. Fitzmahan's new rig."

"Come over to my house Saturday. My folks are away."
"What are we going to do?"
"I thought we could raid the liquor cabinet."

Sometimes children need to ask *"Do you have any money?"*

"Boy, I'd really like to have that tape."
"Do you have any money?"
"No, but if you distract the guy up front, I could sneak away with it."

And sometimes children need to ask several questions before they have enough information:

"Are you doing anything after second period today?"
"No, why?"
"I need you to help me out."
"What do you need?"
"I want you to help me when I see that new kid David."
"What do you want me to do?"
"I want you to talk to him while I tackle him from behind."

Step #2
Name the trouble.
(Key words—"That's . . .")

Naming the trouble helps to point out both to you and to the troublemaker that this is serious business. Using the legal term for the trouble often makes an effective statement:

"Let me fill your glass."
*"I have to drive later; that's **driving under the influence**."*

"Let's smash Mrs. Santorino's new tape deck."
*"That's **vandalism**."*

"Let's punch out Nguyen's lights for getting an A on that test."
*"That's **assault**."*

"Let's take that 6-pack up to the bluff."
*"That's **possession**."*

You don't **have** to use the legal term; use whatever is comfortable for you. At least say *"That's illegal."* We'd like you to be familiar with the legal terms, though, because sometimes it's easier to see the consequences of doing something illegal, as opposed to doing something merely "fun." Legal terms vary from state to state, so you might want to check with your local law enforcement agency.

(Use the Familygram, "Naming the Trouble," at the end of this chapter.)

There are other kinds of troubles besides legal troubles:
▶ family troubles, like leaving a chore unfinished to play basketball with a friend
▶ school troubles, like cheating on a test
▶ health troubles, like taking an unknown chemical substance

▶ "inner" troubles, troubles that make you feel rotten inside, like making fun of somebody

Name whichever trouble is most important to you, and whichever is most likely to influence the troublemaker. Your child can say "That's wrong" or "That's against my family's rules" or whatever is appropriate to the situation.

Step #3
Identify the consequences.
(Key words—"If I did that . . .")

You've asked questions and figured out that there's trouble, and you've named the trouble. Now you're ready to identify the consequences. What are you risking by getting into trouble? It's obvious what could happen if you took to the road with too much alcohol in your system:

"Carla, if I drank any more, I wouldn't be able to drive. I might get into an accident, smash the car, I could even kill myself or somebody else. And even if I did manage to make it home safely, I'd feel lousy because I took an unnecessary risk."

The impulsive act takes on a much greater meaning when we look at what follows the act.

J ust as there are different kinds of trouble, there are different kinds of consequences of getting in trouble—for children as well as for adults:

▶ **legal consequences,** such as being hauled into juvenile court trouble—breaking windows ("If I did that, I'd get a criminal record.")

▶ **family consequences,** such as loss of privileges and of trust trouble—smoking a cigarette after agreeing not to ("If I did that, my Mom and Dad would never trust me again.")

▶ **school consequences,** such as poor grades or expulsion trouble—cheating ("If I did that, I'd flunk the test *and* the course.")

▶ **health consequences,** such as becoming addicted or getting into a drinking/ driving accident trouble—smoking ("If I did that, I'd just end up getting sick.")

▶ **"inner" consequences,** such as feeling stupid or ashamed or guilty trouble—getting drunk before a football game

("If I did that, I'd feel like I could never show my face around here again.")

Step #4
Suggest an alternative.
(Key words—"Instead why don't we . . .")

S o far, we've been responding negatively: "No, that's trouble." "No, bad things will happen if I do that." What now?

"Listen, Carla, I'll try the drink another time. Instead why don't we get me some ginger ale, and you can tell me about your new job."

Suggesting an alternative lets the other person know that you still want to be friends, still want to have fun. You're rejecting the act, not the person. Children need to know which fun, safe, legal, and inexpensive alternatives they can suggest to a friend.

T ake a look at the agenda for the next family meeting. On page 64 write down alternatives to trouble in the spaces provided. Use these as a basis for family discussion. You can make it easier for your children by letting them know which

alternatives you would support.

Step #5
Move it, sell it, and leave the door open.
(Key words—"If you change your mind . . .")

Let's get back to Carla. She's been dying to get you to taste her concoction, and you tell her you'd rather go get a ginger ale—not a real exciting alternative on the face of it. But you can *sell* your alternative:

"Listen, I want to hear all about your new boss. You mentioned before that she expects you to carry a heavy work load."
"Carla, I'm sure you'd rather have me drink ginger ale and live to see another day than to make your punch my last drink ever."
"Come into the kitchen, pour out a glass of the punch, and freeze it for me."

Children can sell their alternatives, too:

"Come on, I dare you to go one-on-one with me in basketball. I'll even spot you five points." **(Challenge)**
"Hey, everyone's going to be skating. I bet Beverly will be there." **(Social reward)**
"Listen, this video is incredible.

Alternatives

▶ going swimming
▶ playing basketball, tennis, or handball
▶ watching TV
▶ helping each other with homework or a school project
▶ going skating or skateboarding
▶ going to the library
▶ making a snack
▶ going for a bike ride
▶ listening to music
▶ taking a hike somewhere

Unbelievable Tales in Family Drug Prevention:
The Fateful Date

 diary found in the ruins of Pompeii indicates that Agrippina Aurelius of Ostia was the first known practitioner of Refusal Skills ("Artes Refusenda"). She practiced the steps by herself for 24 years, waiting in vain for a family member or friend to ask her to get in trouble. Years after her husband Galba passed away, Ms. Aurelius continued to coach herself in case of trouble, but eventually grew despondent. Finally, in the year 79 she was invited by a Roman consul to an orgy at which wine was likely to be served. "That's against my personal rules," she said proudly from memory. "If I did that, I'd feel terrible about myself, and I have to live with me, not you. Instead why don't we go to Mt. Vesuvius? I hear the skiing is marvelous this time of year." The consul relented; Ms. Aurelius stayed out of trouble, kept her friend, and never had a better time.

You'll love it, I guarantee it." **(Promise of fun)**

Carla is still holding the punch, and you're telling her about freezing it for you. There's something else you can do to put pressure on Carla. You can **move**. When you practice this skill, and when you use it, we want you actually to move away from the person who's trying to get you in trouble. Think about it: If you start to move away, who's under pressure to make a decision? Carla. She's the one who's got to decide whether to continue standing there talking to the pitcher of punch or to follow you into the kitchen.

Let's say Carla **still** isn't convinced. What do you do then? What you do then is leave, but leave the door open. You let the other person know that **you've** decided what **you're** going to do; the other person can join you or not.

"Carla, if you change your mind, I'll be in the kitchen."
"If you change your mind, I'll be practicing shots on the court."
"If you change your mind, I'll be making chocolate-chip cookies."

Using *Refusal Skills®* With Groups
Sometimes a **group** of people tries to get you in trouble. This can easily happen to children in school. In that situation, your child shouldn't try to take on the whole group. The most effective thing to do is to take aside the person with whom you have the best relationship. Use the skill with **that** person. If it doesn't work, leave. Maintain the control.

Using *Refusal Skills®* Under Pressure
There's one more type of situation to talk about when someone is trying to get you in trouble. Let's return to the party:

Carla: ". . . I wouldn't want anyone else to try it before you gave it your official okay. Let me fill your glass!"
You: "Carla, that's trouble for me; I'd be driving under the influence. If I drank any more, I wouldn't be able to drive. I could—"
Carla: "Oh, you could drive home with your eyes closed! Listen, just take a—"
You: "But—"
Carla: "—little bit. One glass, that's—"
You: "Wait, I—"
Carla: "—all, and then I'll give you some coffee . . ."

What happened? You didn't have a chance to use the skill. Carla didn't let you get a word in. Now what?

When someone pressures you like this, you have to make the person stop and listen to you. A good way to do this is to say the person's name, pause, say "Listen to me," then pause again to make sure you have the person's attention. You *must* stay calm. You'll be surprised at how effective this is. Once you've got the person's attention, then you can continue using the skill.

Carla: "Oh, you could drive home with your eyes closed! Listen, just take a—"
You: "Carla. Carla, listen to me. (pause) We're talking about driving drunk. I could get in a terrible accident—"
Carla: "You won't get in an accident! I'm telling you, just a little bit—"
You: "Carla. Are you going to listen to me? (pause) I *could* get in an accident. And I could get my driver's license taken away. Instead why don't we find me some ginger ale and you can explain to me why you think you're being overworked."

T hose are the five steps, plus how to respond to groups and how to respond under pressure. Your family can help each other learn *Refusal Skills*® by being "troublemakers," and then by giving each other the key words for each step. Another way to practice is to sign each other's "I Stayed Out of Trouble" cards. If Dad tried to get Jeremiah into trouble, and Jeremiah used the skill successfully, then Dad signs Jeremiah's card. The first person to get five signatures on their card in a week wins a prize.

Look over the agenda, and good luck learning the skill!

In this chapter, "Avoiding Trouble," you've read about how to say no to drugs. Now you'll hold a family meeting to learn how to keep your friends, have fun, and stay out of trouble, and teach the skill to your family.

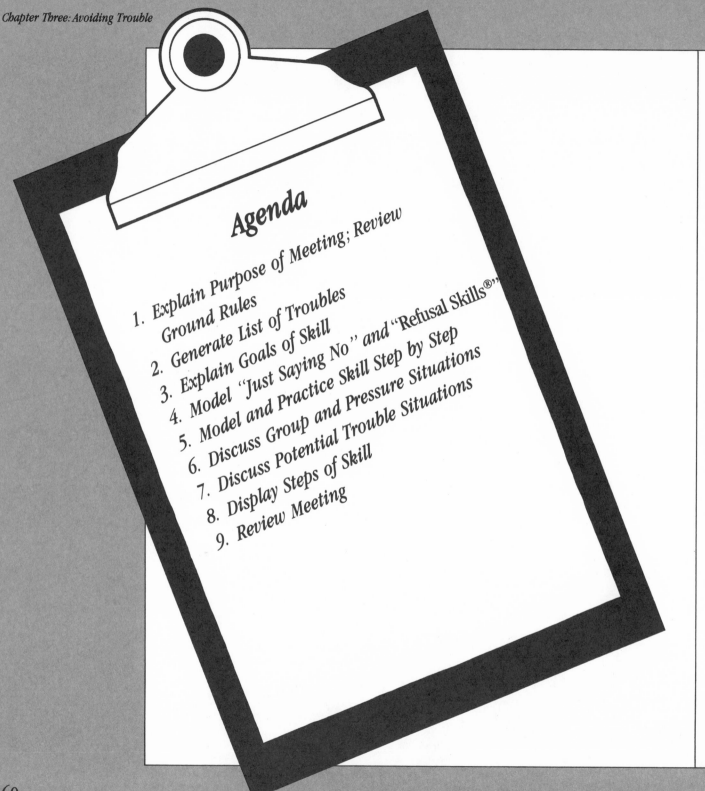

Agenda

1. Explain Purpose of Meeting; Review Ground Rules
2. Generate List of Troubles
3. Explain Goals of Skill
4. Model "Just Saying No" and "Refusal Skills®"
5. Model and Practice Skill Step by Step
6. Discuss Group and Pressure Situations
7. Discuss Potential Trouble Situations
8. Display Steps of Skill
9. Review Meeting

For this meeting you'll need the following:

▶ *Familygram, "Troubles"*
▶ *Familygram, "Refusal Skills®"*
▶ *Familygram, "Naming the Trouble"*
▶ *your suggested alternatives filled out on page 64*
▶ *Familygram, "Alternatives to Trouble"*
▶ *Familygram, "Keep Your Friends, Have Fun, and Say No to Drugs!"*

Teaching a Skill Reminders:

1. Model the steps one at a time.
2. Coach family members who want to learn the skill.
3. Give feedback.
4. Practice.
5. Reward your child.
6. **Have fun!**

1 Explain Purpose of Meeting; Review Ground Rules

Ask for someone to take phone messages so that the meeting won't be interrupted. Say that you're glad everyone could come to the meeting, and that this meeting will be about staying out of trouble.

Review the ground rules:

▶ Everyone gets a chance to talk.

▶ One person talks at a time and doesn't get interrupted.

▶ It's okay to say what you feel.

▶ No one **has** to talk.

▶ Everyone has to listen.

▶ No one puts down anyone else.

▶ _____

▶ _____

▶ _____

Talk about one or two incidents when you got into trouble because you didn't know how to say no to a friend. Maybe you did someone a "favor" that turned out to be more than you originally bargained for. Maybe when you were younger someone persuaded you to smoke. Explain that you got into trouble not because you were "bad" but because you didn't have the skills to refuse. Point out that it's still difficult for you to say no to your friends without feeling that you'll make them mad at you.

2 Generate List of Troubles

Using the Familygram, "Troubles," make a list with your child of different things your child might be asked to do which would be trouble. Some examples:

▶ smoking a cigarette

▶ stealing something

▶ cheating on a test

▶ spray-painting the side of a building

▶ hurting someone

You'll be using this list as a base from which to draw examples for practicing the skill.

3 Explain Goals of Skill

Tell the family that you'd like their help practicing the skill of how to stay out of trouble with your friends, and that after you feel comfortable using the skill you'd like to help them learn it, too. If your child expresses a strong desire to learn the skill now, then use your judgment as to how much to teach. Explain that the goals of the skill are the following:

▶ keep your friends

▶ have fun

▶ stay out of trouble, especially with drugs

4 Model "Just Saying No" and *"Refusal Skills®"*

Model "just saying no" to a friend. Ask a family member to play the role of your friend who invites you to have a beer. Say "No!" and get up and walk away. Point out that you might stay out of trouble just saying no, but you also might end up losing quite a few friends. Now ask the same family member to again invite you to have a beer. This time use the skill (You won't need to do Step #1). Emphasize that using *Refusal Skills®* helps you not only to stay out of trouble, but also to keep your friends and have fun.

5 Model and Practice Skill Step by Step

Model the skill, step by step, and ask family members what they think. Use the Familygram, *Refusal Skills®*, as an aid.

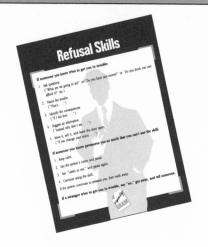

STEP #1.
Ask questions.

(Say to the person: "What are we going to do?" or "Do you have any money?" or "Do you think you can afford it?" etc.)

Tell your family that the first step in the skill is to ask questions. You ask questions to find out if there's going to be trouble. Read the first example to your family:

Troublemaker: *'Let's go over to my house after school."*

You: ***"What are we going to do there?"***

Troublemaker: *"Well, my folks are away."*

You: *"So?"*

Troublemaker: *"So, I thought we'd break into the beer."*

Explain that you can stop asking questions now, because you know there's trouble. Read the next example to your family:

Troublemaker: "Boy, I really want *that candy!"*

You: ***"Do you have any money?"***

Troublemaker: *"No, but I thought you could keep the guy at the counter busy while I swiped the candy."*

Again, explain that you can stop asking questions, because you know there's trouble. Have family members think of trouble situations, and then try to get each other in trouble. Ask everyone to think of what might be trouble situations for your child, too, and use those for examples when you're teaching the rest of the skill.

STEP #2.
Name the trouble.

(Say to the person: "That's . . .")

Tell your family that you should name the trouble as soon as you know what it is. Explain that there are different kinds of trouble, but that you should use the legal name if there is one, because often the legal name sounds serious enough to make the troublemaker reconsider.

(Use the Familygram, "Naming the Trouble," at the end of this chapter.)

Mention other types of trouble:

▶ family trouble, such as violating family guidelines

▶ school trouble, such as cheating on a test

▶ health trouble, such as using an unknown chemical substance

▶ "inner" trouble, such as breaking a promise of confidentiality

Practice the first two steps.

STEP #3.
Identify the consequences.

(Say to the person: "If I did that . . .")

Explain that there are many consequences for getting into trouble:

▶ legal consequences, such as being hauled into juvenile court

▶ family consequences, such as loss of privileges and of trust

▶ school consequences, such as demotion and expulsion

▶ health consequences, such as becoming addicted or getting into a drinking/driving accident

▶ "inner" consequences, such as feeling stupid or ashamed or guilty

Get your child used to the idea of consequences by playing "If I did that . . ." For example:

▶ If I tossed a rock through a window in my neighbor's house, what would happen?

▶ If I started chewing tobacco around the house, what would happen?

▶ If I yelled at my boss, what would happen?

Alternatives

_____

_____

_____

_____

_____

_____

_____

_____

_____

_____

Emphasize that all acts have consequences, and that identifying the consequences beforehand may make you think again about the act. Take turns playing troublemaker as you practice the first three steps, using as many different kinds of consequences as you can think of.

STEP #4.
Suggest an alternative.
(Say to the person: "Instead why don't we . . .")

Explain to your family that when you suggest something else to do, you're telling your friend that you're saying no to the trouble, but not to the friend. Use the alternatives to trouble you wrote down earlier as a basis for discussion.

Now use the Familygram, "Alternatives to Trouble," to generate a bigger list.
Practice the first four steps.

STEP #5.
Move it, sell it, and leave the door open.
(Say to the person: "If you change your mind . . .")

Explain that you might have to sell your alternative, but that, even if your friend doesn't agree, you can still leave the door open for later. When you practice this last step, help the person actually move away from the trouble situation.

6 Discuss Group and Pressure Situations

When you feel that your family is confident using the skill, discuss special situations:

▶ When more than one person is trying to get you into trouble, take aside the person you feel closest to, and use the skill with that person.

▶ When someone is pressuring you so much that you can't get a word in, say the person's name, pause, say "Listen to me," pause again, and continue using the skill. If you can't make the person listen, then walk away.

7 Discuss Potential Trouble Situations

Practice with each other by "trying to get another person in trouble." Discuss potential situations in which each family member might want to use the skill. Also discuss ways for your child to get out of tough trouble situations, for example, a secret word your child can use on the phone. Perhaps your child is at a friend's house and is asked to drink with a friend. Your child could call you, use the secret word, and you would know to ask your child and the friend over to your house to participate in an alternative activity.

8 Display steps of *Refusal Skills*®

Display the steps of *Refusal Skills*® where everyone can see them, or make a copy for each person to person to keep nearby.

9 Review Meeting

Review what you've done in this meeting, and ask if anyone has any ideas how to make the next meeting even better. Set a time for the next meeting, select a person to be in charge of the next meeting's game or refreshments, and end with a game or refreshments. Display the Familygram, "Keep Your Friends, Have Fun, and Say **No** to Drugs!"

KEEP YOUR FRIENDS, HAVE FUN, AND SAY *NO* TO DRUGS!

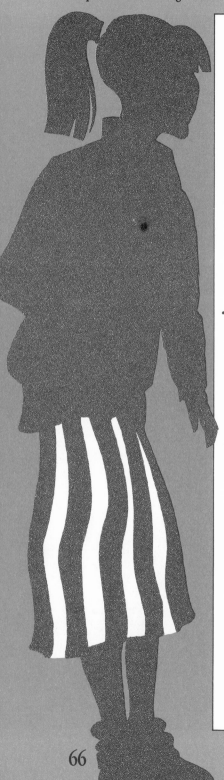

Other Activities for *Avoiding Trouble*

Use these activities as further opportunities for your children to become involved with the family, to learn new skills, and to be rewarded for participating.

1. "What Do You Say?"

This is a fun way to practice *Refusal Skills®*. Each family member thinks of a tough situation for someone else to get out of using *Refusal Skills®*. For example, "Okay, Dad, I'm your boss, and I'm driving you to a meeting out of town. We're on the highway, and I say, 'Hey, there's some beer in the back. How about breaking a couple out. Give me one, and take one for yourself.' What do you say?" Or, "Carolyn, make believe I'm the guy you've been dreaming about for a month, and now I'm asking you out to a party. The only problem is, the party's at the house of this guy who's got a reputation for being a little wild. So I say, 'Well, Carolyn, what time should I pick you up?' What do you say?"

The family can help the person using the skill by cueing the key phrases. If a family member has a problem getting out of the situation, then you can "freeze," and discuss alternatives.

2. Ads for Alternatives

First the family thinks of different things to do that are fun, safe, legal, and inexpensive. These are activities that are offered as alternatives when someone tries to get you into trouble. Family members should have their own lists, because each has personal tastes about what is fun. Then everyone writes, draws, and presents an advertisement for their activity. For example:

The Thrills!
The Spills! The Skills!
Dazzle Your Friends!
Enjoy The Scenery!
Get Some Exercise!
Meet New People!

Go Roller Skating!!

Feel the wind in your hair! Be able to stop on a dime! Amaze your friends with your speed and your cleverness! Take a special person! Take the whole crowd! All you need are your skates!

The purpose of this activity is to get children thinking about how to sell their alternatives. Often we like to do things without realizing why. When children become used to *describing* those things positively, then they can more easily sell them to someone who's trying to get them in trouble.

3. Keep Them Coming — Ways to Generate Alternatives

It's good to keep up a list of fun, safe, legal, and appropriate alternatives to getting in trouble. Think of new activities that your child hasn't tried yet, too. Some of these activities your family can do together; others you can encourage your child to do with a friend, so that each can support the other. There are several fun ways to come up with alternatives:

▶ *Popcorn* — This is best played with at least four or five people. The game is simple. The people who have to come up with alternatives sit down on chairs. When you point to a person, that person has to come up with a fun, safe, legal, and appropriate alternative to getting in trouble within, say, five seconds (You can gauge the time to whatever seems to make the game more fun). Say "Instead why don't we—" and point to people at random. If the person comes up with an alternative, you repeat "Instead why don't we—" and point to someone else. Whoever can't come up with an alternative in the allotted time has to jump up, like popcorn. The last person to "pop" wins.

▶ *License Plates* — When you're riding in the car, point to a license plate and say the name of someone in the car. The person whose name you say has to come up with an alternative activity starting with whichever letter appears first on the license plate, for example, "raking leaves" for RCD 109, or "volleyball" for VA 9412.

▶ *Chain* — This is played like the game "Geography." The first person starts with an alternative, for example, "listening to music." The second person has to think of an alternative beginning with the last letter of the previous alternative. "C" is the last letter of "listening to music," so the second alternative might be "camping." The third

alternative might be "golf," and so on, forming a "chain" of alternatives. If someone is stuck, then that person can "challenge" the last person to have come up with an alternative. If you challenge your daughter, for example, because you can't think of an alternative beginning with the letter "b," and she says "baking cookies," then you're out, and the rest continue to play. However, if she can't think of a "b," either, then she's out, and the rest continue to play. Try to stay away from one-word answers—"fishing," "reading," "gardening"—or else you'll be stuck on "g" for a long time.

4. Troublemakers

One way to practice saying no is to try to get a family member "in trouble" and see if that person uses *Refusal Skills*® correctly. Make a rule that no one can try to get another person in trouble more than, say, once a day. If you succeed in being the troublemaker, then you get a point. If you don't succeed—that is, if the other person uses the skill correctly—then that person gets a point. You can present an award to the family member with the most points at the end of a week.

You can be a "troublemaker" in a lot of different situations:

▶ in the car—"Hey, Dad, we're late, let's go faster!"
▶ in the kitchen—"Let's just rinse these dishes and say we washed them!"
▶ in the park—"Why don't we take that bicycle? No one's around, and I know I can break the lock!"
▶ in a restaurant—"Come on, let's just have dessert! I'm not hungry enough for dinner!"

> " . . . When you're riding in the car, point to a license plate and say the name of someone in the car. The person whose name you say has to come up with an activity starting with whichever letter appears first on the license plate . . ."

Emphasize that the point of this game is *not* to get in trouble, and if someone fails to use the skill correctly, then the other person should say the correct responses.

5. Teaching *Refusal Skills*®

Encourage your child to teach *Refusal Skills*® by showing how to "coach" someone else. Your child can learn the skill even better by teaching it to another person. That person can be anyone who wants to learn, for example, a classmate, neighbor, or relative. When the person your child has taught can show you how to "avoid trouble" by using the skill, you can reward both of them.

6. Keep Them Out of Trouble!

People get into trouble all the time, trouble they might have avoided had they known how to use *Refusal Skills*®. Some of these people are characters in TV shows or newspaper comics. Get together and "rewrite" a panel or two from the Sunday comics section, or discuss a TV show in which someone was pressured by a friend to do something which got them both in trouble. Suggest that your child actually draw the cartoons, with the character mouthing the appropriate steps of the skill. You may want to take a situation from a TV show and act it out, with you playing the character trying to get your child's character in trouble.

Troubles

1. _____

2. _____

3. _____

4. _____

5. _____

6. _____

7. _____

8. _____

Refusal Skills®

If someone you know tries to get you in trouble:

1. Ask questions.
("What are we going to do?" or "Do you have any money?" or "Do you think you can afford it?" etc.)

2. Name the trouble.
("That's . . .")

3. Identify the consequences.
("If I did that . . .")

4. Suggest an alternative.
("Instead why don't we . . .")

5. Move it, sell it, and leave the door open.
("If you change your mind . . .")

If someone you know pressures you so much that you can't use the skill:

1. Keep calm.

2. Say the person's name and pause.

3. Say "Listen to me," and pause again.

4. Continue using the skill.

If the person continues to pressure you, then walk away.

If a stranger tries to get you in trouble, say "no," get away, and tell someone.

Naming the Trouble

Trouble	Legal Name
Buying a 6-pack of beer	Possession of alcohol
Buying marijuana	Possession of a controlled substance
Drinking and driving Smoking marijuana and driving	Driving under the influence
Stealing candy, clothing, etc., from a store	Shoplifting; theft
Breaking a car window Spray-painting a fence or wall	Vandalism
Going into a neighbor's garage without permission	Trespassing
Slashing car tires	Property damage
Taking a car for a joy ride	Auto theft
Hitting a schoolmate	Assault
Setting a fire behind a garage	Arson
Pulling the fire alarm unnecessarily	Malicious mischief
Accepting a stolen radio from a classmate	Possession of stolen property

(Legal terms may vary from community to community.)

FamilyGRAM

Alternatives to Trouble

1. _____
2. _____
3. _____
4. _____
5. _____
6. _____
7. _____
8. _____
9. _____
10. _____
11. _____
12. _____
13. _____
14. _____
15. _____
16. _____
17. _____

KEEP YOUR FRIENDS, HAVE FUN, AND SAY NO TO DRUGS!

Chapter Four
Managing Conflict:
How to Express and Control Your Anger

Rough day . . . traffic . . . hot . . . unexpected lecture by boss . . . neighbors' dog at 2 in the morning . . . unpaid credit card bill . . . funny noise from the carburetor . . . four new gray hairs . . . news bulletin about Middle East crisis . . . no kisses from spouse in last three days . . . and—**your daughter is tying up the telephone when you're expecting a call from out-of-town relatives and if they don't get through to you "sometime this evening" you'll have to call them and it'll be long distance and more expense and what is she talking about that's so important—**

Family members get upset with one another. That's normal; you expect conflict when people live together. What's bad is when families don't **manage** their conflict: They lose control, and say or do things they later regret. Sometimes family members get so angry that they forget they love one another. Children may begin to resent their parents because they feel it's hopeless to please them. If the conflict within the family becomes overwhelming, these children may turn to their peers for the approval, respect, and support they feel they're not getting from their families. If you let anger get in the way of keeping family bonds strong, then your children are at greater risk to leave the family—emotionally if not physically—and at greater risk to use drugs.

In this part of the book we're going to teach you two skills:

▶ **how to express your anger**
▶ **how to control your anger**

We know that on occasion you're going to get angry with your children, but there are ways of expressing that anger which are better than others. If you express your anger constructively, then your children are more likely to understand why you got angry and to work with you to avoid it the next time. They're also going to see you working hard on your own behavior to make the family stronger. For some children, particularly the ones who feel that *they're* always having to do the work, that's a welcome change.

Perhaps an even more important skill is how to *control* your anger. Sometimes you're just too upset to express anger constructively, or you're upset about something unrelated to your family. This skill will teach you how to control that anger until you're able to express it constructively.

You can discuss the skill "How to Express Your Anger Constructively" at your next family meeting. Ask your family to help you learn the skill. Remember, this is a skill *you* need to work on to make your family stronger. After you learn it yourself, in a later meeting you can help teach it to whoever else is interested. Follow the same procedure with the skill "How to Control Your Anger."

Two warnings. First: Skills take practice. You won't change overnight. But we think that after a few weeks of using these skills you'll begin to see a real difference in how you relate to the rest of your family—and how they relate to you. As a result your children will feel more involved in the family, and they'll be reducing the risk of getting into trouble with drugs.

Second warning: These family meetings are for all of you to strengthen family bonds, not to rehash old arguments and get into shouting matches about who's right and who's wrong. The skills of expressing and controlling your anger are intended to prevent just that. So try to use the skills even as you're holding the meeting.

How to Express Your Anger Constructively Expressing your anger constructively addresses the following risk factors:

family management, by decreasing the negative consequences of anger and by helping your child receive only fair, moderate, consistent, and appropriate punishment

alienation, rebelliousness, and lack of social bonding, by helping your child understand why you're upset and see your viewpoint and by maintaining family bonds even when family members are very angry

antisocial behavior in early adolescence (if your child learns the skill), by teaching your child how to express strong feelings without getting into a fight

The skill has three steps. Each step has a few KEY WORDS you say to the person you're upset with. Let's take one step at a time.

If someone makes you upset:
▶ **Step #1.**
Tell the person how you feel.
▶ **Step #2.**
Identify the specific event that made you feel that way.
▶ **Step #3.**
Explain why that specific event made you feel that way.

First, consider some situations which have made you upset in the past. Let's say your son is doing something which is making you angry. Maybe he's talking back to you. Maybe he came home late from school. Maybe he broke something valuable. What other situations upset you? What incidents have occurred in the past in which you got angry at a family member and didn't handle the situation too well?

Take a look at the next family agenda. On page 89 write down a few of the incidents we've been discussing. You can use those during the meeting as examples for practicing the skills.

Step #1
Tell the person how you feel.
(Key words—"I'm . . .")

You may be angry, you may be disappointed, you may be frustrated, you may be feeling something else. We think it's important to identify the feeling both to yourself and to the other person. For example, if your 10-year-old son came home late from school, your feeling may have been more worry than anger. Knowing that you were worried might help your son understand why coming home late from school was wrong and increase the chances that he won't do it again. On the agenda under #3, write down some words to describe how you felt when the situations you just listed upset you.

Step #2
Identify the specific event that made you feel that way.
(Key words—"I'm _____ because . . .")

Be specific. Don't talk about what "always" happens, or what happened some other time. Stick to the situation. If you make your comments too general, then your child may feel that you're being unfair, or that you can never be pleased.

Use the situation to try to change the specific behavior, not your child's entire personality. Here are a few examples:

"I'm angry because you went to that movie and you said you wouldn't."
"I'm disappointed because you drank that can of beer from the refrigerator."
"I'm anxious because you didn't study for that test today."

Write down the examples that apply to you under #3 of the agenda.

Step #3
Explain why that specific event made you feel that way.
(Key words—"When you _____, I felt . . .")

Explaining why the event made you feel the way you do lets your child know that there's a reason behind your feelings, and your child may have more incentive to help solve the problem. Here are some examples:

"When you went to that movie after you said you wouldn't,

How to Express Your Anger Constructively

If someone makes you upset:
1. Tell the person how you feel.
2. Identify the specific event that made you feel that way.
3. Explain why that specific event made you feel that way.

How to Control Your Anger

1. Stop.
2. Think about what will happen if you lose control.
3. Ask yourself why you're really angry.
4. Reduce the anger.
5. Reward yourself.

I felt that I couldn't trust you.''

"When you drank that can of beer from the refrigerator, I felt that you didn't respect our family rules."

"When you didn't study for that test today, I felt that you didn't care about getting good grades."

Notice that the explanation is short. You don't need to justify your feelings, because that can lead into an argument. You need only to explain why you feel the way you do.

You've told your child how you feel, what made you feel that way, and why you're upset. What happens now?

It depends. If you're angry because your daughter is talking too long on the telephone, you can use the skill, and ask her to hang up. The problem is solved. But if this was the third time this week you told your daughter you were angry because she was talking on the phone too long, then the problem is yet to be solved. You need to deal with it.

This skill–how to expess your anger constructively—helps you get to the point at which you're ready to solve problems. Ultimately, you will want to try to fix whatever it was that got you upset. For now, let's focus on expressing anger in a way that prevents the situation from getting worse.

How do you practice this skill? At the next family meeting your family can help you. They can remind you of situations that have made you upset in the past. They can pretend to get you angry so that you can run through the steps with them. They can give you the key words for each step. In the agenda for the next family meeting, we'll show you how you can explain this skill to your family.

Before we do that, however, do you remember the example we gave you at the beginning of the chapter? You'd had a rough day, you were expecting a call, and your daughter was on the phone. You were ready to explode. What do you do then? What do you do when you're too upset to express your anger constructively? What do you do when you're just about to lose control? In those situations you can use another skill—"How to Control Your Anger."

How to Control Your Anger

Sometimes you're so angry you can't see straight. Other times you may be upset about something unrelated to a family member who's just an innocent bystander. These are the times when you need not to express your anger, but to *control* it. Once your anger is under control, you can express it to the appropriate person. Controlling anger addresses the following risk factors:

family management, by decreasing the negative consequences of anger and by helping your child receive only fair, moderate, consistent, and appropriate punishment

alienation, rebelliousness, and lack of social bonding, by helping your child understand why you're upset and see your viewpoint and by maintaining family bonds even when family members are very angry

antisocial behavior in early adolescence (if your child learns the skill), by teaching your child how to prevent getting into a fight by controlling anger

The skill has five steps. If someone makes you upset:

▶ **Step #1.**
Stop.
▶ **Step #2.**
Think about what will happen if you lose control.
▶ **Step #3.**
Ask yourself why you're really angry.
▶ **Step #4.**
Reduce the anger.
▶ **Step #5.**
Reward yourself.

Again, let's take the skill one step at a time. The words following each step are KEY WORDS you say *to yourself* to remind yourself what to do.

Think of some recent incidents that *really* upset you—incidents that caused you to lose control. Maybe you slammed a door in your spouse's face; maybe in the heat of anger you said something mean to your child. As you did before, turn to the meeting agenda and, under #5, write down a few incidents to use as examples. Now let's begin discussing the steps of the skill.

Step #1
Stop.
(Key words—"I'm getting angry.")

This is probably the most important step. When you recognize that you're becoming so upset that you're about to lose control, you must stop. How do you know you're losing control? Learn to recognize your **anger signs.** Everyone has different signs. Here are some:

▶ your voice rises
▶ your voice trembles
▶ your face gets red
▶ your temples throb
▶ your hands shake
▶ your jaw tightens
▶ you breathe faster
▶ you feel hot
▶ you wish everyone would just leave you alone
▶ you find it difficult to concentrate

What are **your** anger signs? People you've been upset with may be able to identify some if you can't. It's important to recognize your anger signs, so that you can use the rest of the skill.

Step #2
Think about what will happen if you lose control.
(Key words—"If I lose control . . .")

H ow do you feel when you lose control? How does your child feel? How does losing control affect the relationships within your family and between your family and others? Sometimes picturing what will happen if you lose control serves as a "brake." You probably don't want to lose control, don't want to say or do hurtful things to the members of your family. When you see the consequences of *losing* control, you're more likely to *keep* it.

You're about to blow up at your son for losing an expensive pen you bought him for school. *"If I lose control, then I'll end up feeling even worse."*

You're about to blow up at your daughter for watching TV with her friends instead of taking the garbage out. *"If I lose control, then she'll be humiliated in front of her friends."*

You're about to blow up at your whole family because you're impatient to leave the neighbors' house. *"If I lose control, then they won't invite us back."*

When you consider the consequences of your actions, you're more likely to reconsider your actions.

Step #3
Ask yourself why you're really angry.
(Key words—"The real reason I'm angry is . . .")

Y ou may have a good reason for getting angry at a family member. Then again, you may not. That family member may just be in the wrong place at the wrong time. You may really be angry at your boss, or upset about your finances. But it's usually safer—in the short run—to yell at your child than your boss. And it's easier to express anger at your child for not doing her homework than to deal with a problem like not having enough money to pay the bills. So you may take it out on the family member—unless you stop to ask yourself why you're really angry.

Your son is playing the stereo really loud, but now you think about that phone call you got from your brother last night. *"The real reason I'm angry is that my brother's getting divorced."*

It's true that your daughter didn't take out the garbage, but now you think about what happened when you took a look at your paycheck this afternoon.

"The real reason I'm angry is that I didn't get that raise I expected."

But let's not forget, sometimes your anger is directed at precisely the right person: *"The real reason I'm angry is that she's on the telephone when she's supposed to be studying."*

Step #4
Reduce the anger.
(Key words—"I need to cool down. I'm going to . . .")

You've stopped yourself from losing control, and you've identified the source of your anger. Now you'd like to reduce your anger. If it's appropriate, you can reduce your anger by expressing it constructively to whomever you're upset with. But, as we just noted, it may not be appropriate; you may really be angry at someone other than your family member. Furthermore, whether or not you have a good reason for getting upset at a family member, you may be in no shape to express yourself constructively. You need to take time out and cool down.

 ow do you cool down? You might need only to count to 10 and take a

> "Children who engage in (misbehaving in school, skipping school, and getting into fights with other children) are at increased risk for engaging in another socially undesirable behavior, drug abuse."

Unbelievable Tales in Family Drug Prevention:
The Phall of a Pharaoh and the
Delay of a Skill

t is 1582 B.C., and Ikhnotep IV, one of the moodiest Pharaohs of Egypt, is restless. In the past two years alone, he has hit at the Hittites, assailed an army of Assyrians, and invaded Thrace thrice. Now, on a hot summer afternoon full of mosquitoes and irritating labor disputes, the ruler feels a surge of anger ready to overwhelm him. Fortunately his wife, Queen Shethsput, recognizes his primary anger sign, which is ordering wars on neighboring provinces. This time Shethsput is prepared. First, she gets him to call back those of his soldiers still within shouting distance. Next, she gets him to admit that if he loses control, the Egyptian forces might be defeated in battle. After some reflection, Ikhnotep admits that he's really upset about his sister, who eloped the previous week with an asp-tamer. Shethsput massages her husband's head to reduce his anger. Then, as a reward, she offers him a

sweet pink confection made to resemble homegrown cotton.

Ikhnotep can't get enough of the new treat; it literally melts in his mouth. He begins controlling his anger at least twice a day, identifying anger signs like "feeling a little warm" and "getting an unfriendly thought." Soon peace is reigning over Egypt, Ikhnotep is gaining a great deal of weight, and slaves can be seen stifling giggles. One day Shethsput comes across some graffiti chiseled in a stone. She thinks it says, "The Pharaoh is a Phatty," but cannot make out all the hieroglyphics. Nevertheless, she knows that although Ikhnotep has got control of his anger, he has lost control of his diet. Recalling the slim husband she was forced to marry, Shethsput is upset. Getting angry at a Pharaoh, however, even if he's your husband, can mean a quick trip to the

next life, so she controls her anger by eating the cottony candy.

he following summer the royal couple journey to Babylon to attend a commemoration of the death of Hammurabi. There Ikhnotep finishes off his supply of candy and gets a toothache. It hurts him so much that he starts to curse the memory of Hammurabi. This is a mistake, because the Babylonians take their idols seriously. They charge the royal guard. Ikhnotep and Shethsput are too fat to flee; they are caught and forced to participate in "The 50,000-Shekel Pyramid," a primitive Babylonian torture.

The fall of Ikhnotep and his Queen sets back the skill of managing conflict for at least a thousand years, until in 530 B.C. a Phoenician chemist discovers a way to make cotton candy sugar-free.

few deep breaths. Or, if you're **really** upset, you might try any of the following:

▶ walk or jog for 20 minutes
▶ take a shower or bath
▶ read something funny
▶ lie down and put on some music
▶ think about a happy time you spent with the person who's making you angry
▶ call a friend
▶ do a chore
▶ sit down with a magazine and a refreshing beverage
▶ write a letter to someone you haven't seen in over a year
▶ find a quiet place and try not to think of anything for a little while

Write down ways you could cool down on page 93 of the family meeting agenda. Use them as examples when you're explaining this step. Then your family can help you fill out the Familygram, "Ways to Cool Down," by making other suggestions.

After you cool down, you may find that there's no reason to be upset with a family member. If you do need to express your anger, however, you can now use the skill to do so constructively.

Step #5
Reward yourself.

(Key words—"I did a good job! I'm going to . . .!")

You've controlled your anger. You've helped to maintain the bonds in your family. Congratulations! But you'll probably need more than our congratulations in order to motivate yourself to continue using the skill. Here are some things you can do for yourself:

▶ take yourself to lunch or to a movie

▶ buy yourself something you want but really don't need (within reason)—a kite, a bar of fancy soap, a radio with earphones, a plant

▶ spend an evening with a friend

▶ block out a time alone to exercise

▶ try something new—cook without a recipe, read someone a story, make up a game

▶ make a list like this one, put it in a jar, and use it when you've successfully controlled your anger

As you did with ways to cool down, come up with ways to reward yourself, and list them on page 94 in the family agenda. Then your family can help you fill out the Familygram, "I Deserve It!"

How you can hold your family meeting, and describe "How to Express Anger Constructively" and "How to Control Anger" to your family. Again, explain that you're trying to learn these two skills, and ask your family to help you. They can help you practice controlling your anger the same way they helped you practice expressing your anger:

▶ They can remind you of situations that have made you upset in the past.

▶ They can pretend to get you angry so that you can practice the steps.

▶ They can give you the key words for each step, even though, when you're controlling your anger, you're saying the words to yourself.

▶ They can leave you little notes in places where you will easily find them—in your car, in your medicine cabinet, etc.—reminding you to follow the steps because they care for you. These notes can be attached to a list of the steps of the skills.

Look over the agenda, and good luck learning the skills!

In this chapter, "Managing Conflict," you've read about how to express and control your anger. Now you'll hold a family meeting to learn how to express anger in a way that will maintain communication and help to solve the problem that caused the anger. You'll also learn to recognize anger signs, and cool down before you make the situation worse.

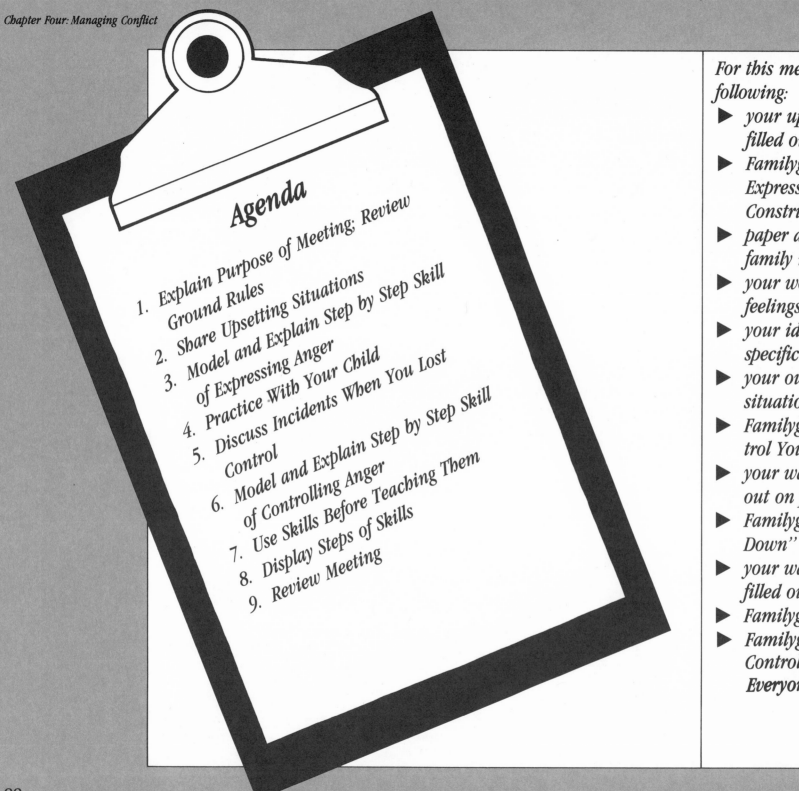

Agenda

1. Explain Purpose of Meeting; Review Ground Rules

2. Share Upsetting Situations

3. Model and Explain Step by Step Skill of Expressing Anger

4. Practice With Your Child

5. Discuss Incidents When You Lost Control

6. Model and Explain Step by Step Skill of Controlling Anger

7. Use Skills Before Teaching Them

8. Display Steps of Skills

9. Review Meeting

For this meeting you'll need the following:

► *your upsetting situations filled out on page 89*

► *Familygram, "How to Express Your Anger Constructively"*

► *paper and pencil for each family member*

► *your words to describe your feelings filled out in #3*

► *your identification of the specific events filled out in #3*

► *your out-of-control situations filled out in #5*

► *Familygram, "How to Control Your Anger"*

► *your ways to cool down filled out on page 93*

► *Familygram, "Ways to Cool Down"*

► *your ways to reward yourself filled out on page 94*

► *Familygram, "I Deserve It!"*

► *Familygram, "Staying In Control Is Good For Everyone's Health!"*

1 Explain Purpose of Meeting; Review Ground Rules

Ask for someone to take phone messages so that the meeting won't be interrupted. Say that you're glad everyone could come to the meeting, and that you'll be discussing how to express your anger and how to control your anger as ways to manage conflict in the family. Review the ground rules:

▶ Everyone gets a chance to talk.

▶ One person talks at a time and doesn't get interrupted.

▶ It's okay to say what you feel.

▶ No one **has** to talk.

▶ Everyone has to listen.

▶ No one puts down anyone else.

▶ _____

▶ _____

▶ _____

Talk about one or two recent incidents when you got angry at a family member and didn't handle the situation too well. Use the examples from those you wrote down earlier.

What happened in each situation? Did you solve the problem? How did you feel after you "handled" the situation? How did the other person feel?

2 Share Upsetting Situations

Ask family members to write down some situations which upset **them**, other than reactions to someone else's anger. Briefly discuss what there is in common among the upsetting events. Impress upon your family the importance of everyone working together to express anger constructively.

3 Model and Explain Step by Step Skill of Expressing Anger

Tell the family that you'd like

I Got Angry When . . .

_____

_____

_____

_____

_____

_____

_____

_____

_____

_____

_____

their help in learning two different skills. The first skill is how to express your anger in a way that's fair and that keeps the family close. Remind them of the family goals all of you came up with before and how expressing your anger constructively will help achieve those goals. Describe the skill, step by step, and ask family members what they think. Use the Familygram, "How to Express Your Anger Constructively," as an aid; you can find it at the end of this chapter.

How to Express Your Anger Constructively

If someone makes you upset:

1. Tell the person how you feel. ("I'm . . .")

2. Identify the specific event that made you feel that way. ("I'm _____ because . . .")

3. Explain why that specific event made you feel that way. ("When you _____, I felt . . .")

If you're so upset you feel you're losing control, then use the skill "How to Control Your Anger."

Step #1.
Tell the person how you feel.
(Say to the person: 'I'm . . .")

Read the examples to your family:
"I'm angry . . ."
"I'm disappointed . . ."
"I'm frustrated . . ."
Then read your own examples:

_____

_____

_____

Ask each person to refer to the times when they were angry, or disappointed, or frustrated. Discuss the differences between the feelings and how one might lead into another.

Step #2.
Identify the specific event that made you feel that way.
(Say to the person: "I'm _____ because . . .")

Read the examples to your family:
"**I'm mad because** you haven't

done your homework and it's 9:00."
"**I'm disappointed because** you said you'd clean the kitchen and you didn't."
"**I'm frustrated because** you did so poorly on the test."
Continue to use your own examples:

_____

_____

Step #3.
Explain why that specific event made you feel that way.
(Say to the person: "When you _____, I felt . . .")

Read the examples to your family:
"**When you didn't do your homework, I felt** that you're taking advantage of my letting you watch TV instead of being responsible for school."

*"**When** you said you were going to clean the kitchen and then didn't, **I felt** that I couldn't trust your word, and I end up having to do the work."*

*"**When** you did poorly on the test, **I felt** helpless, because I know you can do better but I don't know how I can help you improve your grades."*

Explain to the family that the third step leads you to a point where you can begin to solve the problem.

4 Practice With Your Child

Using the same examples, ask your child to help you practice the skill by giving you the key words for each step. Ask how your child would feel if you got angry that way. You might want to set up a practice schedule, with one family member "getting you angry" each day.

5 Discuss Incidents When You Lost Control

Now talk about one or two recent incidents when you got really angry at a family member and lost control:

_____

_____

_____

Don't make excuses for your behavior, and don't blame anyone; just talk about what happened because you lost control in those situations.

For example, you might say to your daughter:

"Do you remember last week when I came home and your room was a mess? I started screaming, and then I told you you couldn't go out after school for two weeks. You spoke about seven words to me the next two days, and I think I suffered more than you did."

Or, you might say to your husband:

"Remember a couple of paydays ago when I got mad after you bought those new shoes? I took my purse and flung it against the wall, only it bounced off and broke the vase we bought on our anniversary. I felt stupid for losing my temper; plus, the vase cost more than the shoes."

Impress upon your family the importance of everyone working together to control anger.

6 Model and Explain Step by Step Skill of Controlling Anger

Tell the family that sometimes you get so upset that you can't express yourself constructively. Explain that there's another skill that you'd like their help in learning— "How to Control Your Anger." Describe the skill, step by step, and ask family members what they think. Use the Familygram, "How to Control Your Anger," as an aid.

Step #1.
Stop.

(Say to yourself: "I'm getting angry.")

Explain that anger signs tell us that we're getting upset and in danger of losing control. Tell your family what your anger signs are; maybe your face gets red and you feel hot. Say that when you recognize your anger signs, you have to stop, or you'll lose control. Have your family identify their own anger signs.

Step #2.
Think about what will happen if you lose control.

(Say to yourself: "If I lose control . . .")

Read the examples to your family:

You're about to blow up at your son because he accidentally broke your favorite lamp.
"If I lose control, then I'll be just as angry, but I'll feel guilty, too."

You're about to blow up at your daughter because she told you her friend gave her a cigarette.
"If I lose control, then she'll be less likely to tell me the truth next time."

You're about to blow up at your family because they can't decide which restaurant they want to stop at on the highway.
"If I lose control, then it'll spoil the whole weekend."

Discuss what else might happen if you lost control. Use examples from the past, or make up situations. Think about what might happen to you, the person you got mad at, and the family as a whole. Consider long-term as well as short-term consequences. Ask other family members to relate incidents when they lost control. Make the point that losing control doesn't meet anyone's goals or help change troublesome behaviors.

Step #3.
Ask yourself why you're really angry.

(Say to yourself: "The real reason I'm angry is . . .")

Explain to your family that some-times you're angry because of something entirely unrelated to them.

Read the examples to your family:

"The real reason I'm angry is the heating bill that just came in the mail."

"The real reason I'm angry is because I just heard that my friend George got in an automobile accident."

"The real reason I'm angry is because I had a rough day at work."

Ask your family to suggest other reasons which might make you angry or upset.

Remind them that many times you **are** really upset with the family member. Even if you did have a rough day, for example, you might be really angry at your child for neglecting chores.

Step #4.
Reduce the anger.

(Say to yourself: "I need to cool down. I'm going to . . .")

Explain that one way of reducing anger is to express it. Add that if you feel you have things under control, then you'll use the skill with them to express anger constructively. But if you're too upset to express the anger, or if you're upset because of some other reason, then you'll need to cool down first.

Read the examples to your family:

"I need to cool down. I'm going to take a walk."

"I need to cool down. I'm going to lie down and put on some music."

"I need to cool down. I'm going to take a shower."

Read the examples you wrote before.

How Can I Cool Down?

_____

_____

_____

_____

_____

_____

_____

_____

Rewards

_____

_____

_____

_____

_____

_____

_____

_____

_____

_____

Using the Familygram, "Ways to Cool Down," ask everyone to help you make a list of ways you could cool down, and display it where you're likely to see it.

Step #5.
Reward yourself.

(Say to yourself: "I did a good job! I'm going to . . .!")

Explain that you want to learn this skill because you think it will help the family to remain close and to achieve some of the goals you talked about before. Add that one way to help you learn the skill is to reward yourself when you've used it well.

Read the examples to your family:

"I did a good job! I'm going to take myself to a nice place for lunch!"

"I did a good job! I'm going to relax tonight!"

"I did a good job! I'm going to spend an evening with my friend Susan!"

Again, use the examples you wrote before.

Using the Familygram, "I Deserve It!," make up a list of other ways to reward yourself, and display that list, too.

Ask your family to help you learn this skill the way they agreed to help you learn the skill of expressing your anger constructively. They can suggest situations which might make you upset, and they can give you the key words to say for each step.

7 Use Skills Before Teaching Them

If family members want to learn the skills themselves, be sure that you've been using the skills for at least one week and that you're confident using them before trying to teach them to others.

8 Display Steps of Skills

Display the steps of the skills where everyone can see them.

9 Review Meeting

Review what you've done in this meeting, and ask if anyone has any ideas how to make the next meeting even better. Set a time for the next meeting, select a person to be in charge of the next meeting's game or refreshments, and end with a game or refreshments. Display the Familygram, "Staying In Control Is Good For **Everyone's** Health!"

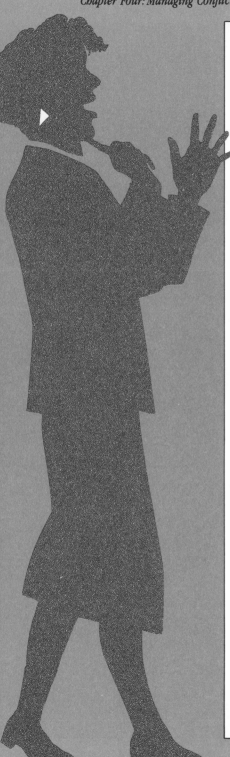

Other Activities for *Managing Conflict*

Use these activities as further opportunities for your children to become involved with the family, to learn new skills, and to be rewarded for participating.

1. Log Rolling

This activity isn't quite what it sounds like. It's important for families to keep track of the times they *don't* manage anger constructively, so that they can see what went wrong. In this activity, family members keep a log of when they lose control. Each slip of paper stands for a time when a family member lost control. It could include information like:

▶ Person's Name:
▶ Day:
▶ Time:
▶ What Happened:
▶ Results:
▶ Ways It Could Have Been Handled Better:
▶ What to Look for Next Time:

Just before a family meeting, family members roll their logs up and put a rubber band around them. In the meeting the logs are put in a pile, and everyone takes turns choosing a log and reading it aloud. The family can discuss each situation— maybe someone has a different perspective—and ways to improve it. After a while, family members can see which steps of the skills they need to work on most.

2. Reward Jars

All family members write what they would consider personal rewards on slips of paper, like listening to music for one undisturbed hour (You may want to set a cost or time limit). Everyone should have the same number of rewards, without duplicates. Family members then place these slips of paper in Reward Jars or Reward Boxes, and use them when they've successfully controlled their anger or expressed it constructively. The family can even decorate the Reward Jars. No one, however, can take a reward out of the Reward Jar without the permission of another family member. Time can be set aside at family meetings to write more rewards. A variation of this is that when one person uses the Reward Jar, then all family members can use theirs: Everyone in the family benefits when anyone in the family controls anger.

3. TV Conflict Search

The family watches a TV show together, maybe a detective or adventure show. When it's over, they discuss ways that the characters handled conflict. How could the characters have done it differently? How would that have affected the rest of the show? The family can also talk about how much violence can be avoided by controlling anger.

4. Scrolls

When family members practice expressing and controlling their anger, the emphasis sometimes is placed on "negative" situations—what makes us upset, and often *who* makes us upset. "Scrolls" is an activity which focuses on the positive side of family relationships—what we like about each person. The activity itself is simple: Each family member has a scroll—name on top, personally decorated, it's up to the individual. Everyone writes comments on everyone else's scroll. The comments respond to one basic question: "What is it about this person that I like?" You can write as many comments as often as you decide. The scroll becomes a record of happy thoughts for the person to consult at any time.

You don't have to use scrolls for this activity; you can use note cards or notebooks. The point is for all family members to recognize that they have positive qualities which are valued by other family members. This expression of mutual love and caring contributes greatly to family bonding.

5. Sell the Skills

Why should families learn to manage conflict? Why is it important for them to express and control their anger? What is it about these two skills that accomplishes those objectives? As we've mentioned before, your family will be more apt to learn and use these skills if they understand the importance of doing so. Take turns "selling" the skills. Pretend that you're a parent who's never heard of the skills, and ask your child to persuade you to learn them. Your family might discover reasons for using the skills that you didn't realize before. You may want to pretend selling the skills in a variety of ways—in a TV commercial, a newspaper editorial, or a speech before a group. How does your presentation change depending on the medium and on the audience?

6. How I Feel

"How I Feel" wheels are "pie charts" divided into "wedges" labeled with feelings like "happy,"

"tired," "hurt," "excited," "thoughtful," and "depressed." You make them by cutting out circular sheets of paper or cardboard, dividing the circle into as many different sections as you want, and labeling the sections with a heavy marker or crayon. The wheels—either one for each member of the family or one for the entire family—should be displayed where everyone can see them. If you use one family wheel, then each member of the family should have a marker—a certain-colored thumbtack, a pin with a little flag in it, a magnet, etc.—to place on the wheel. "How I Feel" wheels let people in the family know how everyone else is doing at any particular time. For example, you might notice that your son has placed his marker in the "hurt" section; this might prompt you to ask him what's wrong. Your wife may come home from work and place her marker in the "tired" section; this might be a warning to give her a little time to herself. You can reserve a section in the center of the wheel or outside the wheel for neutral feelings. "How I Feel" wheels help to manage conflict by giving family members added information about others' moods. The idea is for them to spur communication, not to substitute for it, and to realize that some conversations—for example, those requiring important decisions—should be undertaken when the participants aren't in strong negative moods.

> "... The family watches a TV show together, maybe a detective or adventure show. When it's over, they discuss ways that the characters handled conflict ..."

How to Express Your Anger Constructively

If someone makes you upset:

1. Tell the person how you feel.
   ("I'm . . . .")

2. Identify the specific event that made you feel that way.
   ("I'm _____ because . . . .")

3. Explain why that specific event made you feel that way.
   ("When you _____ , I felt . . . .")

If you're so upset you feel you're losing control, then use the skill "How to Control Your Anger."

How to Control Your Anger

If someone makes you upset:

1. Stop.
   ("I'm getting angry.")

2. Think about what will happen if you lose control.
   ("If I lose control . . .")

3. Ask yourself why you're really angry.
   ("The real reason I'm angry is . . .")

4. Reduce the anger.
   ("I need to cool down. I'm going to . . .")

5. Reward yourself.
   ("I did a good job! I'm going to . . .!")

Ways to Cool Down

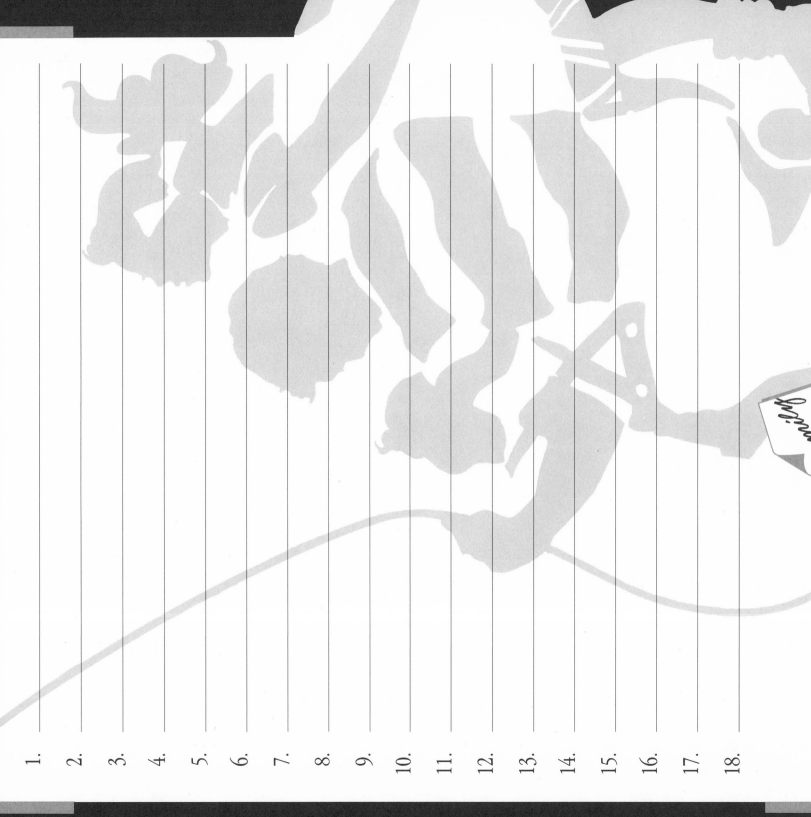

Family GRAM

1.
2.
3.
4.
5.
6.
7.
8.
9.
10.
11.
12.
13.
14.
15.
16.
17.
18.

I Deserve It!

I did a good job! I'm going to:

1. _____

2. _____

3. _____

4. _____

5. _____

6. _____

7. _____

8. _____

9. _____

Family GRAM

STAYING IN CONTROL IS GOOD FOR EVERYONE'S HEALTH!

Chapter Five
Involving Everyone:
How to Strengthen Family Bonds

Throughout this book we've encouraged you to do three things to strengthen the bonds in your family and reduce the risk of your child's getting in trouble with drugs:

▶ provide your child with opportunities to become involved in the family

▶ teach your child skills to contribute successfully to the family

▶ reward your child for successful involvement

Let's say you've held your family meetings the way we've suggested. Your child has participated in the activities and learned some of the skills. Maybe you've even rewarded your child for learning *Refusal Skills*®. Now we'd like you to think about how to provide a **continual** atmosphere in which your child feels involved, successful, and appreciated.

As children enter the teenage years, it's important to prepare them for adult roles—to help them learn to make good decisions, to manage money, to be **responsible**. In this chapter we're going to show you some ways to increase your child's involvement in the day-to-day operation of your family, and we're going to continue to encourage you to look for opportunities to do things **together**, as a family. This is where the real bonding occurs; this is where your child will come to believe, "Yes, I do matter in this family," and "Yes, I am committed to this family." This is the atmosphere we're talking about when we urge you to provide a positive alternative to drugs. The family that involves their child meaningfully will be reducing the risks of their child's abusing drugs.

Look at the list below. Do you recognize any of these people?

▶ the helper
▶ the clown
▶ the purchaser
▶ the janitor
▶ the enforcer
▶ the decision maker
▶ the planner
▶ the troublemaker
▶ the bookkeeper
▶ the victim
▶ the bungler
▶ the spokesperson

They're not really people; they're roles. A small family could easily assume all of the roles we just listed, and often does. The problem with roles is that they're limiting: Once we're in them, people think we can perform only certain tasks, and forget we can do any others. But a family has to perform many tasks to survive, and many more to thrive. Think about dinner.

Tasks before eating:

1. decide what to eat
2. buy the food
3. prepare the meal
4. set the table

Tasks after eating:

5. compliment the cook
6. clear the table
7. wash the dishes and utensils
8. dry and put away the dishes and utensils

Who performs each of these eight tasks in your own family? Is it the same person each time—the "decision maker" for #1, the "purchaser" for #2, and so on? Is the person who decides what to have for dinner the same person who decides where your family takes vacations? Does the same family member always shop for food, as well as for furniture and anything else the whole family uses? Does **anyone** in your family compliment whoever made dinner? Finally, does the same person always do the same chores around the house?

Who does what in your family? You may have some very good reasons for why one person always cooks, one person always takes out the garbage, one person always plans the family budget. Or, you may be locked into roles that are preventing your child from making more meaningful contributions to the family. Children **can** feel like an important part of the family, when we expand their roles to give them responsibility. Expanding family roles addresses the following risk factors:

family management, by increasing your child's opportunities to contribute to the management of your family by becoming involved and making decisions

alienation, rebelliousness, lack of bonding to society, by increasing your child's commitment to the family

antisocial behavior in early adolescence, by teaching your child how to become involved in positive family behaviors and rewarding your child for doing so

friends who use drugs, by strengthening family bonds so

that children will be less likely to associate with friends whose behavior could threaten those bonds

early first use of drugs, by increasing your child's rewards for doing well in order to decrease your child's chances of looking for rewards from drugs

Your family can expand family roles together. The process has five steps.

▶ **Step #1.**
Make a list of the tasks necessary for your family to operate comfortably.
▶ **Step #2.**
Note who currently performs each of those tasks.
▶ **Step #3.**
Find out what family members want to do and what they are able to do, especially with help at first.
▶ **Step #4.**
Reassign tasks, and choose monitors for each task.
▶ **Step #5.**
List the consequences of performing and of not performing the tasks well.

We'll describe the steps to you now, and your family can do them at your next family meeting. We'll provide you with

Familygrams at the end of this chapter to help you. Let's start with Step #1.

Step #1
Make a list of the tasks necessary for your family to operate comfortably.

Besides activities associated with work and school, most families perform tasks which fall into these general areas:
▶ governance tasks—making rules and decisions affecting the family as a whole
▶ maintenance tasks—cleaning, cooking, sewing, etc.
▶ financial tasks—budgeting, purchasing, paying bills, etc.
▶ health tasks—trying to prevent and taking care of medical and dental problems

Your family may find other general areas useful to make your list, for example, transportation tasks or social tasks. Use what works best for you. List all important tasks in each area that need to be performed, and how often they need to be performed:
▶ determining rules for alcohol use—
  every year

▶ taking out the kitchen garbage when full—usually every other day
▶ balancing the checkbook—every month
▶ making dental appointments—every six months for each person

In your next family meeting agenda, on page 118, draft a list of important tasks and how often they need to be performed. This will form the basis for the list your family makes out later.

Step #2
Note who currently performs each of those tasks.

Beside each task, write the name of the family member who currently performs that task. Do this on page 118 on the meeting agenda. For example:
▶ pays the monthly bills—Mom
▶ washes the breakfast dishes—
  Mom, Dad, Sheila, Elliot
▶ washes the dinner dishes—Sheila

You can learn some interesting things about how your family is managed by doing this exercise:

Expanding Family Roles

1. Make a list of the tasks necessary for your family to operate comfortably.
2. Note who currently performs each of those tasks.
3. Find out what family members want to do and what they are able to do, especially with help at first.
4. Reassign tasks, and choose monitors for each task.
5. List the consequences of performing and of not performing the tasks well.

Decisions For Young Children

Consider the following decisions: For which ones can your children begin to take more responsibility? Which ones can they make with a little help?

make decision alone	make decision with help	
		1. when I go to bed
		2. what I eat for breakfast
		3. where the family goes for vacation
		4. which TV shows I watch
		5. which music I listen to
		6. what clothes I wear
		7. which movies I see
		8. what to name pets
		9. which sports I play
		10. which chores I do
		11. how I get my hair cut
		12. who my friends are
		13. what I do after school
		14. how I spend my money
		15. where I go to school

Are there tasks for which no one is responsible? Are several people responsible for performing the same task? Is one person responsible for too many tasks?

Step #3
Find out what family members want to do and what they are able to do, especially with help at first.

Here's where you can tell if you've been pigeonholing family members into performing certain tasks just because everyone else thought that's what they should do. We've talked about providing opportunities for your child to contribute meaningfully to the family. What opportunities have you been providing? Think about the major areas we suggested: governance, maintenance, financial, and health. Has your child outgrown certain tasks? Is your child bored with other tasks? Isn't it possible that, with a little help, your child could learn to contribute in all these areas?

▶ governance—deciding what the family could do together on a Sunday

▶ maintenance—vacuuming the living room

▶ financial—budgeting a personal allowance for clothes, entertainment, etc.

▶ health—keeping records of when each family member last visited the doctor and dentist

"What about the tasks that no one wants to do, like washing the bathroom floor?"
There are probably enough of these tasks to go around, so that everyone gets at least one task they want, and no one gets stuck with all the unpleasant tasks. You may want to change tasks every so often. Another alternative is to allow family members to trade tasks on their own. One person may love mowing the lawn but hate washing dishes, and the other person may feel just the opposite.

"It doesn't make any sense to let my child cook; my child doesn't know a colander from a calendar."
If you agree that it's important for your child to learn how to cook—and you may not agree—then teach your child. Start with something easy, model it step by step, and give a lot of feedback and encouragement when your child does it. Reward your child for successfully learning the task.

"I work all day, and when I come home I'm just too tired to clean the bathroom."
Remember, we said that you should find out what family members are **able** to do. You may be unable to perform a task because you don't have the skill, or because you don't have the knowledge, or because you don't have the time or energy. Think about which maintenance tasks require little time or energy, like setting the table or emptying the wastebaskets. Maybe the whole family could do the cleaning together on a Saturday morning. Be flexible!

Step #4
Reassign tasks, and choose monitors for each task.

Now it's time to assign tasks to each person. You may find that only a few new assignments need to be made. On the other hand, the family routine may be in for quite a lot of changes. This is a time for **patience.** People are learning new skills, and everyone performs tasks in a slightly different way from everyone else. Don't assume that everyone knows that wiping the table, stove, and countertops is part of doing the dishes, or that vacuuming includes cleaning behind the furniture and then moving things back in place and putting the vacuum cleaner away. You may have to teach that!

One way to improve the quality of the tasks and to further include your child in family activities is to assign "checkers" for certain tasks. For example, if the task of mowing the lawn twice a month falls to Armando, then maybe his sister Julia could check to make sure the task is performed. Or Armando can ask his father each month if he remembered to set aside part of his paycheck for "family fun activities."

Step #5
List the consequences of performing and of not performing the tasks well.

In an earlier part of the book, we talked about setting expectations for drug use, and listing positive consequences for your expectations being met and negative consequences for your expectations not being met. We said that giving rewards for successful participation in the family contributed to family bonding. You can do the same thing here:

► task—scrubbing the bathtub once a week
► responsibility—Harris

► checker—Valetta
► positive consequences— after 10 consecutive times, a barbecue party for his friends
► negative consequences— for missing 3 times, no TV for a week

Everyone needs to be aware of both the positive *and* the negative consequences. The more the consequences fit both the person and the task, the greater the likelihood of success. Remember that positive consequences can be non-material things, too, like compliments and expressions of love and caring:

"You really did a good job on the dishes! I'm proud of the way you're contributing!"

"I know how hard it is for you to take care of your little brother, and I love you for pitching in when we need it."

Look over the agenda for your next family meeting. By increasing the opportunities for your children to contribute to your family every day, by teaching them skills to contribute in new ways, and by rewarding them for successful participation, you're strengthening the family bonds your children will depend on later. Good luck!

Unbelievable Tales in Family Drug Prevention:
The Baker's Daughter

Jedediah Crumb, a New York baker in the early 1900's, doted on his daughter Sophie. Every day he would bring her up to the shop and let her play with the flour or knead the dough. "Sophie," he would often say, "someday this all will be yours." When Sophie was 11½, Crumb astonished his friends by giving her the coveted job of Head of Batter Composition. "I love you, Sophie," he told her that morning while easing a caraway rye out of the oven. "And I know you'll do right by me." Sophie worked hard, encouraged by the steady hand of her father and propelled by her own instinctive talent. After a year of experimenting with yeast derivatives, she developed a way of doubling the bulk of all Crumb's products while using only 10% more ingredients. Profits soared. Crumb rewarded his daughter by opening up the Sophie Crumb Bakery in Newark, New Jersey, and before he retired owned 38 bakeries and outlets in the mid-Atlantic states and western New England. He had turned a family business into a successful corporation, merely by taking the time to expand his family rolls.

In this chapter, "Involving Everyone," you've read about how to strengthen family bonds. Now you'll hold a family meeting to learn how to divide up tasks so that your child can contribute more meaningfully to the family.

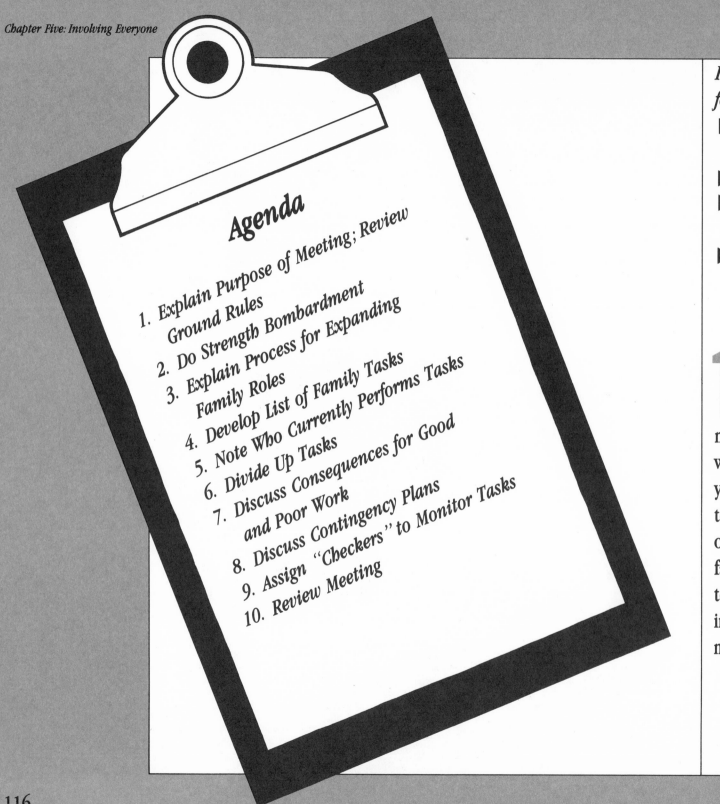

Agenda

1. Explain Purpose of Meeting; Review Ground Rules
2. Do Strength Bombardment
3. Explain Process for Expanding Family Roles
4. Develop List of Family Tasks
5. Note Who Currently Performs Tasks
6. Divide Up Tasks
7. Discuss Consequences for Good and Poor Work
8. Discuss Contingency Plans
9. Assign "Checkers" to Monitor Tasks
10. Review Meeting

For this meeting you'll need the following:

▶ *your list of important family tasks filled out on page 118*
▶ *Familygrams, "Family Tasks"*
▶ *paper and pencil for each family member*
▶ *Familygram, "We're All Involved In Making Our Family Strong"*

1 Explain Purpose of Meeting; Review Ground Rules

Ask for someone to take phone messages so that the meeting won't be interrupted. Say that you're glad everyone could come to the meeting. Explain that one of the primary ways to make the family stronger and more resistant to problems with drugs is by making sure that everyone is meaningfully involved in perform-

ing the everyday tasks of managing the family. Say that you'd like
to look at how those tasks are
currently divided, and then follow
a process suggested in this book
to divide them up in new ways.
Emphasize that you'd like
everyone to decide how to divide
up tasks. Review the ground rules:

▶ Everyone gets a chance to
talk.

▶ One person talks at a time
and doesn't get interrupted.

▶ It's okay to say what you feel.

▶ No one **has** to talk.

▶ Everyone has to listen.

▶ No one puts down anyone
else.

▶ _____

▶ _____

▶ _____

2 Do Strength Bombardment
Point out that you think it's
important for everyone to
become significantly involved in
the family because everyone in the
family has skills as well as the
ability to learn new skills. One way
of showing appreciation for each
other's skills and qualities is to do
a "Strength Bombardment."
Explain that it's important that all
members of the family be aware
that they are loved and valued,
and that Strength Bombardments
help provide that awareness. Ask
for one person to sit in the middle
of a circle, with the others forming
the circle. Everyone else takes
turns telling the person in the
center what they appreciate about
that person. The person receiving
the strength bombardment is
allowed to respond in only one of
three ways: "Thank you." "Thank
you; I agree with that." "Thank
you. That sounds so good I'd like
to hear it again." Then everyone
else takes a turn in the center. It
may be difficult at first to accept
all the compliments, but strength
bombardments usually make
people feel very good about
themselves.

3 Explain Process for Expanding Family Roles
Briefly explain the process
for expanding family roles:

Step #1.
Make a list of the tasks necessary
for your family to operate
comfortably.

Step #2.
Note who currently performs each
of those tasks.

Step #3.
Find out what family members
want to do and what they are able
to do, especially with help at first.

Step #4.
Reassign tasks, and choose
monitors for each task.

Step #5.
List the consequences of performing and of not performing the
tasks well.

Our Family Tasks

What?	How Often?	Who Does It?

4 Develop List of Family Tasks

Share the list of tasks you wrote down which you think necessary for the family to operate comfortably, along with how often the task has to be performed. Use this list as a basis for discussion. Use the Familygrams, "Family Tasks," to compile the final family list.

Explain that you'd like to divide the tasks into the following categories so that everyone has something to do in each category:

- governance tasks—making rules and decisions affecting the family as a whole
- maintenance tasks—cleaning, cooking, sewing, etc.
- financial tasks—budgeting, purchasing, paying bills, etc.
- health tasks—trying to prevent and taking care of medical and dental problems

You may want to start off with only a few important tasks at this meeting, and add to the list at another meeting. Continue to use the Familygrams.

5 Note Who Currently Performs Tasks

Note who currently performs each task, as you wrote in the space provided.

6 Divide Up Tasks

Discuss what family members would like to do and what they are able to do. Go down the list of tasks, and try to make sure

that everyone is responsible for performing at least one task in each category. It's all right to continue with the person who's currently performing the task, but being open to changes will show your child that you're serious about expanding roles. If someone needs help to perform a new task, then note who will be helping that person and what kind of help is going to be provided. Usually the person who had been performing the task is the most likely one to help the person who will be performing the task.

7 Discuss Consequences for Good and Poor Work

Discuss rewards for good work and negative consequences for poor work. Assure your child that no one will be punished for not doing a new task well for an initial "grace period," and that your child will be getting help

learning the task during this period. Set a time at which the plan will be reviewed and appropriate changes made. Determine rewards and other consequences.

8 Discuss Contingency Plans

Discuss contingency plans, for example, when someone is sick or out of town or otherwise unable to perform a task. Many families like to have the person responsible for performing the task also responsible for finding a replacement, perhaps in a temporary swap of job duties. You can discuss other options as well, for example, family members getting together to share a task, like planning a menu for the week.

9 Assign "Checkers" to Monitor Tasks

Assign "checkers" to monitor those performing tasks. Display the schedule where everyone can

use it. Offer a lot of encouragement during the first few weeks,
because this is a difficult time for
adjustment.

10 Review Meeting

Review what you've done
in this meeting, and ask if
anyone has any ideas how to make
the next meeting even better. Set
a time for the next meeting, select
a person to be in charge of the
next meeting's game or refreshments, and end with a game
or refreshments. Display the
Familygram, "We're All Involved
In Making Our Family **Strong**."

WE'RE
ALL INVOLVED
IN MAKING
OUR
FAMILY
STRONG.

1. Starting a Tradition

Let your child have a say in planning how your family will celebrate holidays. You can discuss different ideas, and reach a consensus on what type of thing to do—or place to go—on an upcoming holiday. For example:

▶ For New Year's Day, the family discusses plans for the coming year and plays a game or puts together a puzzle after dinner.

▶ For the first day of spring, the family does something related to animals or plants—visits a zoo or aquarium, goes to a movie about animals, works in the garden, etc..

▶ For Independence Day, the family has a picnic in the evening and stays up late to watch the fireworks.

▶ For Election Day, the family does something related to government—reads from and discusses the U.S. Constitution, writes a letter to an elected official, shares information each person has collected about how other governments work, discusses issues and candidates relating to the election, etc..

▶ For Thanksgiving, the family takes food to a food bank.

For birthdays, each family member can write a personal letter to the birthday person. In these letters the family members say what they appreciate about the birthday person, and why the birthday person is special.

2. I Saw Someone Doing Something Good!

This activity acknowledges positive behaviors, and rewards your child for contributing to the family. Hang a piece of poster paper on a door or wall, or reserve space on the message board. Write at the top, "I Saw Someone Doing Something Good!" Tell your family that whenever anyone sees another family member doing something good, that person should write it on the chart and sign it. For example:

▶ *I saw Jay help the neighbor carry his groceries. — Mom*

▶ *I saw Juanita clean up her room without being told. — Ron*

▶ *I saw Dad help Mom with the taxes. — Lynn*

▶ *I saw Jane being real nice to Neal when he was in a bad mood. — Dad*

At your next family meeting, or at dinnertime, you can read the items on the list and discuss them. You may even want to present a special award for the person who did the best thing on the list.

Other Activities for *Involving Everyone*

Use these activities as further opportunities for your children to become involved with the family, to learn new skills, and to be rewarded for participating.

121

> "... Making up 'I Love You' codes is a private way of saying 'I Love You' to a family member ... the code can be a nonsense phrase ... or it can even be a gesture ..."

3. Walk in My Shoes

We said before that it's often appropriate for some family members to perform certain tasks, whether because that person has more time, more ability, or more interest, etc., in the task. Sometimes, however, many tasks get taken for granted. In this activity you show another family member what it's like to do what you do: This can be entertaining as well as educational!

Let whoever pays the monthly bills show everyone else how it's done. Let whoever prepares dinner explain to everyone else the specific procedure required to get the food from the grocery into the mouths of the family members. Let whoever decides what clothing to purchase, where to get it, and how much to spend for it describe to everyone else the decision-making process involved. You can even switch roles for a day!

This activity is a good opportunity for *everyone* to learn about everyone else. Sometimes parents are just as unaware of what children do as children are of what parents do. When family members gain a better understanding of each other's tasks, then the family bonds will be strengthened.

4. The *I Love You* Code

Sometimes family members want to express their love and caring for each other, but for one reason

or another—perhaps they're with a group of people—they're too shy to do so. Making up "I Love You" codes is a private way of saying "I Love You" to a family member. The code can be a nonsense phrase with the same initials, like "It's a Long Yesterday." It can be a short statement, like "You know." Or it can even be a gesture, like three taps on the person's shoulder. The idea behind the "I Love You" code is that no situation should prevent a family member from expressing love to another.

5. Who We Are

This activity emphasizes things that make family members unique as well as things that make the family a cohesive unit. First, each family member fills out an "I" profile. This profile can be a self-drawn picture or a creative design or a fancy way of writing the person's name. All the profiles should answer the same questions. You can make up your own questions, but here are a few suggestions:
▶ What's my favorite animal?
▶ What's my favorite place?
▶ What's my favorite dessert?
▶ What's my favorite sport?
▶ What's my favorite color?
▶ What's my favorite chore?
▶ Who's someone I admire?
▶ What's something I do well?
▶ What's something I wish I did better?
▶ What's something I do for fun?
▶ What's something I do when I feel sad?
▶ What's something I like to do with the whole family?

When everyone is finished with "I" profiles, family members can discuss each one, and note shared answers. Then the family can fill out a "We" profile. Collaborate on a family picture, or a family "crest," or just a nonsense design. Then you can discuss and answer questions like these:

▶ What's our ideal vacation?
▶ What's our favorite time at home?
▶ What's our favorite Sunday activity?
▶ What's our favorite pet?
▶ What was a time we really had to work together?
▶ What was a time we really felt good about ourselves as a family?

Now you can discuss what each of you learned:

▶ What did I learn about myself?
▶ What did I learn about another family member?
▶ What did I learn about the family as a whole?
▶ What is something our family really likes to do together?
▶ What is something our family would really like to do together?

You can repeat this activity throughout the year, using different questions or seeing how your answers change over time.

6. Tell Someone Else

This is a variation of saying nice things to a family member. In this activity you tell someone else something nice about a family member, or the family as a whole. Maybe your son can tell his friend that he's proud of his sister for learning how to swim. Maybe you can tell a co-worker that your spouse went on a diet and is looking great. At the next family meeting, each family member can report on what was said to whom. You may want to make "assignments" so that all family members get something nice said about them.

This is an indirect way of expressing love and caring. Making our feelings "public," communicating our feelings about family members to another person, is a very special way of acknowledging those feelings to ourselves. It also makes family members feel good to know that you think enough of them to tell someone else.

Family Tasks [Governance]

Family GRAM

Governance Tasks (making rules and decisions affecting the family as a whole)

1. Task: _____
   Done how often: _____
   Whose responsibility before: _____
   Whose responsibility now: _____
   Type of help, provided by whom: _____
   Checker: _____
   Reward for doing well: _____
   Negative consequences for doing poorly: _____

2. Task: _____
   Done how often: _____
   Whose responsibility before: _____
   Whose responsibility now: _____
   Type of help, provided by whom: _____
   Checker: _____
   Reward for doing well: _____
   Negative consequences for doing poorly: _____

3. Task: _____
   Done how often: _____
   Whose responsibility before: _____
   Whose responsibility now: _____
   Type of help, provided by whom: _____
   Checker: _____
   Reward for doing well: _____
   Negative consequences for doing poorly: _____

4. Task: _____
   Done how often: _____
   Whose responsibility before: _____
   Whose responsibility now: _____
   Type of help, provided by whom: _____
   Checker: _____
   Reward for doing well: _____
   Negative consequences for doing poorly: _____

Family Tasks [Maintenance]

Maintenance Tasks (cleaning, cooking, sewing, etc.)

1. Task: _____
   Done how often: _____
   Whose responsibility before: _____
   Whose responsibility now: _____
   Type of help, provided by whom: _____
   Checker: _____
   Reward for doing well: _____
   Negative consequences for doing poorly: _____

2. Task: _____
   Done how often: _____
   Whose responsibility before: _____
   Whose responsibility now: _____
   Type of help, provided by whom: _____
   Checker: _____
   Reward for doing well: _____
   Negative consequences for doing poorly: _____

3. Task: _____
   Done how often: _____
   Whose responsibility before: _____
   Whose responsibility now: _____
   Type of help, provided by whom: _____
   Checker: _____
   Reward for doing well: _____
   Negative consequences for doing poorly: _____

4. Task: _____
   Done how often: _____
   Whose responsibility before: _____
   Whose responsibility now: _____
   Type of help, provided by whom: _____
   Checker: _____
   Reward for doing well: _____
   Negative consequences for doing poorly: _____

Family Tasks
(Financial)

Financial Tasks (budgeting, purchasing, paying bills, etc.)

1. Task: _____
   Done how often: _____
   Whose responsibility before: _____
   Whose responsibility now: _____
   Type of help, provided by whom: _____
   Checker: _____
   Reward for doing well: _____
   Negative consequences for doing poorly: _____

2. Task: _____
   Done how often: _____
   Whose responsibility before: _____
   Whose responsibility now: _____
   Type of help, provided by whom: _____
   Checker: _____
   Reward for doing well: _____
   Negative consequences for doing poorly: _____

3. Task: _____
   Done how often: _____
   Whose responsibility before: _____
   Whose responsibility now: _____
   Type of help, provided by whom: _____
   Checker: _____
   Reward for doing well: _____
   Negative consequences for doing poorly: _____

4. Task: _____
   Done how often: _____
   Whose responsibility before: _____
   Whose responsibility now: _____
   Type of help, provided by whom: _____
   Checker: _____
   Reward for doing well: _____
   Negative consequences for doing poorly: _____

FamiGRAM

Family Tasks (Health)

Health Tasks (trying to prevent and taking care of medical and dental problems)

1. Task:
   Done how often:
   Whose responsibility before:
   Whose responsibility now:
   Type of help, provided by whom:
   Checker:
   Reward for doing well:
   Negative consequences for doing poorly:

2. Task:
   Done how often:
   Whose responsibility before:
   Whose responsibility now:
   Type of help, provided by whom:
   Checker:
   Reward for doing well:
   Negative consequences for doing poorly:

3. Task:
   Done how often:
   Whose responsibility before:
   Whose responsibility now:
   Type of help, provided by whom:
   Checker:
   Reward for doing well:
   Negative consequences for doing poorly:

4. Task:
   Done how often:
   Whose responsibility before:
   Whose responsibility now:
   Type of help, provided by whom.
   Checker:
   Reward for doing well:
   Negative consequences for doing poorly:

WE'RE ALL INVOLVED IN MAKING OUR FAMILY _STRONG._

Chapter Six
Moving Forward:
How to Organize a Parent Support Group

We've tried to help you prepare for your child's drug-free years. We hope that you've used family meetings as a springboard to provide your child with more opportunities for becoming involved in your family, to teach your child new skills, and to reward your child for new successes. We've shown you how strengthening the bonds in your family reduces the risks that your child will get in trouble with drugs.

But there's more. You've seen how effective you can be in changing attitudes and behaviors within your own family. Just as you are an effective force within your family, a **group** of parents can be an effective force throughout your community. In the past decade alone, parents have organized hundreds of community groups to increase public awareness about drugs and drug use, to get drug prevention and drug education programs into schools, and to put pressure on local establishments where drugs are commonly used. Parents are supporting each other, and they're learning from each other. You can do so much more when you've got the numbers.

There are other good reasons for organizing a parent group. Discussing drug issues with other parents can help you clarify your own positions on drugs. You can learn different strategies used by other families, and adapt them to your own family's circumstances. And you can get support: Does your child make you feel as if you're being unreasonable about your guidelines for drug use? Does your child tell you that other parents have much more lenient rules about drugs? When you meet with other parents, you can find out.

We said that you can do so much more when you've got the numbers. How do you get the numbers? That's what this final chapter is about. We don't want the last page of this book to be the last effort you make in keeping children safe from drugs. At the beginning of *Preparing for the Drug (Free) Years: A Family Activity Book,* we called this book a tool. We hope we've taught you how to use this particular tool; but a lot of other tools are waiting out there for you to pick up and use, and a lot of other people are waiting out there to use them, too.

Organizing a parent support group can ultimately help reduce every risk factor we've discussed in this book. It can bring you in contact with people who have very similar concerns as you. These parents also have visions for their children. They also take pride in their children's accomplishments. They also want to do the right thing.

Here is a basic four-step process for organizing a parent support group:

► **Step #1.**
  Get together informally with a small group of parents.
► **Step #2.**
  Select leaders to share responsibility.
► **Step #3.**
  Arrange to meet at a specific time and place.
► **Step #4.**
  Do something together to act on an issue.

As we've done before, let's take one step at a time:

Step #1
Get together informally
with a small group
of parents.

This first meeting could be with friends from your church, or the PTA, or a professional group, or the neighbors on your block, or other members of a parent workshop. Consider the letter on this page as an example.

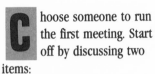hoose someone to run the first meeting. Start off by discussing two items:
► which issues people would like to address
► how to organize the group more effectively

If you take a large sheet of butcher paper and some marking pens to the meeting, you can make a list of issues which people think are important and which they think they can do something about. For example:
► Teenagers are known to smoke marijuana near a local fast-food establishment.
► The middle school has no effective drug education curriculum.
► Police have been too lax in enforcing drinking-driving laws.
► Across the street from the middle school are two billboards advertising cigarettes.

► No one can recognize current drug paraphernalia.
► Not enough people are familiar with local drug treatment resources.
► There is a cocaine "rock house" in the neighborhood.

Brainstorm as many ideas as you can think of. You may find that there are issues that concern the group more than drug abuse—learning about teenage sexuality, preventing child abuse, or finding a safe community center for teenage recreation. After you finish brainstorming, have everyone choose the issues they think are the most appropriate for the group to tackle. One way to do this is by giving everyone three stickers, and have them distribute the stickers next to the issue or issues they prefer. Select the issue with the most stickers to be discussed at your next meeting.

Y ou'll also want to discuss organizational issues—how to enlarge the group; which people in the community might be effective allies or speakers; whether, when, and how to get publicity. Brainstorm names of people who might be interested in joining the group and who

(Date) _____

Dear _____

We're a group of parents who would like to get together with other parents to discuss our concerns about children's exposure to drugs. Recently we've learned three important facts:

*► Most of the children who try nicotine, alcohol, and marijuana do so **before** they enter high school.*
► Studies show that the risks of drug abuse are more than double when children start using these drugs before age 15.
► Parents—acting within their own families and throughout their community—can help reduce the risks of our children's getting into trouble with drugs.

We'd like to share our ideas, to learn how other parents handle some of the difficult questions they face as their children become teenagers. On _____ to discuss these issues at _____ we'll be getting together at _____. We hope you can be there. We'll talk about how we might organize into an effective group and which issues we'd like to address. We might decide to address issues other than drug abuse as well. We'll also decide how often we want to meet and who will be responsible for coordinating the meetings.

We, like you, are parents of children who are approaching the peak years of risk for drug problems. We believe that we'll be able to come up with positive, preventive strategies, and maybe even some solutions to problems we're already facing.

We hope to see you there on _____. Please feel free to tell other parents of 9–13-year-olds about the meeting. If you have any questions, call _____ at _____

Sincerely,

Organizing a Parent Support Group:

1. Get together informally with a small group of parents.

2. Select leaders to share responsibility.

3. Arrange to meet at a specific time and place.

4. Do something together to act on an issue.

could help the group. Make up a phone list, and ask each of the parents on the list to suggest other parents who might be interested in joining the group.

Step #2
Select leaders to share responsibility.

Once you've determined what it is you want to focus on, you'll find it helpful to choose someone to coordinate your efforts. Some groups like to select one leader to minimize confusion, and then alternate leaders every few months. Other groups like to divide responsibility between co-leaders so that the burden doesn't all fall on one person. If only one person is chosen, then that person should be willing and able to delegate responsibility. When you choose your leaders, consider the following criteria:

▶ **must have the time to perform the required tasks** Does the person have a job which allows doing other things during the day? which doesn't require a lot of travel? which leaves time for all the activities *besides the group* the person wants to do?

▶ **must have the energy to perform the required tasks** Is the person in good health? able to work for the group after hours?

▶ **must have the ability to perform the required tasks** Is the person responsible? articulate? fair? enthusiastic? organized? able to take the initiative? able to work well with others?

▶ **must have the support to perform the required tasks** Does the person have access to a typewriter? a telephone? a car? people to rely on for assistance?

▶ **must have the desire to perform the required tasks** Is the person a parent of a child about 9–13 years old? concerned about drug abuse? committed to the success of the group?

Step #3
Arrange to meet at a specific time and place.

It's usually an advantage to secure a permanent meeting place, perhaps in a church or a school. That way people who miss one meeting know where the next meeting is going to be held. You can also print flyers in advance which advertise the

meeting. Providing pot luck snacks is often one way of encouraging people to attend. Reaching agreement on a time to meet may be a problem. A weekday evening is usually best, but the most successful groups realize that not everyone will be able to make every meeting. Decide how often to meet: Meeting too often can burn people out quickly. Many groups find that meeting monthly is optimum.

Step #4
Do something together to act on an issue.

When you decide just what it is you're going to do as a group, it's the leader's responsibility to divide tasks, follow up on activities, and be the spokesperson for the group. Take advantage of the enthusiasm you've generated from using this book! Spread your enthusiasm around! You have the incentive of helping the vision you have for your child become a reality. You have the skills we've shown you in this book, and you have the ability to learn more skills. If all of you support each other, you'll succeed in preparing your children for the drug-free years.

Helpful Information

Signs of Drug Use

This book discusses risk factors for teenage drug abuse and ways families can reduce these risk factors. The term "drug abuse" is used because the research which is the basis for this book sought to identify precursors of frequent drug use and of problems associated with drug use. It is clear from that research that starting to use alcohol or other drugs early in the teen years itself increases the risk of problems with drugs. For teenagers, the most prudent course for avoiding drug problems is not to use drugs.

None of the following signs or symptoms are definite proof your child is using drugs. But if several of these signs are present and you have other reasons for being concerned, you should probably check out your suspicions.

1. **Changes in school performance and behavior**—lower grades, absenteeism, discipline problems, loss of interest in school or cocurricular activities like sports or music

2. **Changes in mood or behavior**—moodiness, depression, increased time alone, loss of interest in activities that were important, hyperactivity, anxiety, irritability

3. **Changes in physical appearance**—red eyes, runny nose, chronic coughing, weight loss

4. **Changes in friends**—reluctance to bring friends home, new friends whose parents you don't know

5. **Changes in eating and sleeping habits**—loss of appetite, increased appetite, craving for sweets, insomnia, drowsiness